Never
Lose Hope

Also by José H. Cortés

Nunca Pierdas la Esperanza

Never Lose Hope

JOSÉ H. CORTÉS

Pacific Press®
Publishing Association

Nampa, Idaho | Oshawa, Ontario, Canada
www.pacificpress.com

Cover design by Steve Lanto
Cover design resources from iStockphoto.com / Syldavia
Inside design by Kristin Hansen-Mellish

The author assumes full responsibility for the accuracy of all facts and quotations as cited in this book.

Unless otherwise indicated, Bible quotations are from the New King James Version®. Copyright © 1982 by Thomas Nelson, Inc. Used by permission. All rights reserved.

Scripture quotations marked KJV are from the King James Version.

Scripture quotations marked NIV® are from the HOLY BIBLE, NEW INTERNATIONAL VERSION®. Copyright © 1973, 1978, 1984, 2011 by Biblica, Inc.® Used by permission. All rights reserved worldwide.

The narratives in chapters 5–7 on Joseph and chapter 8 on Daniel have been enriched, paraphrasing *Patriarchs and Prophets* (Nampa, ID: Pacific Press® Publishing Association, 2002) and *Prophets and Kings* (Nampa, ID: Pacific Press® Publishing Association, 2002) by Ellen G. White.

Additional copies of this book are available by calling toll-free 1-800-765-6955 or by visiting http://www.AdventistBookCenter.com.

Library of Congress Cataloging-in-Publication Data
Names: Cortes, Jose H., 1949- author.
Title: Never lose hope : experiences lived in a communist jail ... , and other true and unedited stories / Jose H Cortes.
Description: Nampa : Pacific Press Publishing, 2016.
Identifiers: LCCN 2016040531 | ISBN 9780816361915 (pbk.)
Subjects: LCSH: Cortes, Jose H., 1949- —Imprisonment. | Clergy—Cuba—Biography.
Classification: LCC BR1725.C6854 A3 2016 | DDC 277.291/082092—dc23 LC record available at https://lccn.loc.gov/2016040531

December 2016

Dedication

This book is dedicated to Celia Cortés, the person who has been my companion and support in the happiest moments of my life—but also during my difficult times in a Communist prison. She was and is always there, when I confront the challenges of ministry and face conflicts with the enemies of our faith. Celita my beloved wife—strong and sweet like the sugarcane!

I also have to recognize my support team: José H. Cortés Jr. and Joanne, Josué H. Cortés and Joyce, José H. Cortés III, Nadia Mitchel, Joel Benjamín, and Ema Christine. They are my inspiration.

I love all of you from here to the sun—round-trip!

Thank you a million for what you do. God bless your ministry!

J. H. Cortés
New Jersey Conference

Contents

Introduction

The huge iron doors squeaked behind me; left behind were my freedom; my dear wife, who was expecting our first child; and my distraught parents, who could not fathom the full scope of what was happening. Our community of believers, once again shocked and perplexed at the actions of the Cuban Revolution's so-called People's Courts, asked themselves how it could be that a respectable and honest citizen such as their pastor had been convicted and unfairly cast into prison, without having committed any crime.

Mine was not an isolated case, nor did I suffer the greatest cruelty. In these pages, it is not my intention to swamp the reader with murky bitterness, because truthfully the events never did manage to bring bitterness to my spirit. I do not want to waste ink attacking a decrepit dictator who dedicated his life to creating a model of government that never worked; his great failure is retribution enough. This system set the course for inevitable failure and self-condemnation from the day when it tried to take God out of the picture by arbitrarily enacting a law prohibiting the sharing or dissemination of religious ideas and doctrines outside the immediate confines of the church building.

In effect, this decree suspended the right of all citizens who did not agree with Castro's Communist regime to freely share their faith or creed. It provided the authorities with an effective tool by which to legally imprison any minister or religious person who would not conform to the new state of atheism. This law would never be ultimately successful, and it is never the right of any government, no matter how absolutist, to attempt to force its citizens to abandon their faith and to teach their children that God does not exist.

Equally destructive to the public well-being is the imposition of any form of obligatory religion. In matters of conscience, nobody has the right to legislate, neither rulers, nor kings, nor even the very church. The Creator has given human beings an inalienable right called free will; and without it, life is meaningless. To believe or not to believe is a very personal matter; to try to suppress religious liberty or to impose restrictions upon it violates the most basic rules of life and undermines our peaceful coexistence.

But no, my dear readers, do not worry; I will not yield to the temptation to politicize this work, even though many of the stories I share with you here have been written with a pen dipped in the blood of the heart. But the spirit of this work is not political or polemic. I want only to present before you the facts as they happened and through them to sing the victories of good will, faith, hope, and love, which—even in the midst of misery itself—far outweigh in greatness the effects of arbitrariness, abuse, and crime. I humbly recognize that the dividing line will be very thin, and that is one of the reasons why I have resisted publishing these testimonies for years. However, I have finally decided to listen to the requests of numerous Spanish-speaking, English-speaking, and French-speaking friends, who have heard me tell of these experiences in my lectures and sermons. They have told me that I must publish my story, as it will be a blessing to believers and nonbelievers alike. But above all else, I want to obey the urgings of my conscience, which is loudly insisting that the world must learn about the lives of those who still exist, even if their existence is denied them! Men and women who, forgotten by their own families and ignored by the world, have become heroes of faith, sustained in their sufferings only by the Christian hope! Several of those whose names are written indelibly on my mind may still be alive, but I do not know where they are imprisoned today. Communication has been practically impossible. Even so, I have before me an old notebook whose withered and yellowed pages are full of memories; what is scribbled on those pages has been crying out to me with an insistent voice, pleading for me to be these people's mouthpiece. They oblige me to overcome the inertia of my pen and, at last, write. In this way, they have stimulated painful memories that have been struggling to come to light for years, while I have fruitlessly sought to repress so many of those memories during numerous years.

Today I am fulfilling my duty to convey these testimonies, which for obvious reasons, do not reveal the true identity of the various individuals, including the central character with whom I closely identify. I do not mention these people by their real names in order to protect their families and friends who may still live on that cloistered island. I have also decided, out of respect for the families and the church, not to mention the names or the negative actions sadly committed against those left to suffer abandonment by several high-ranking religious leaders who presided over the church at that time in history. I recognize that they experienced a natural fear for their safety and that they were concerned with their own survival. Clearly, they felt the need to maintain their positions of leadership or even their personal freedom, which later some of them also lost; but I never again felt respect or admiration for them, even to this very day. (God forgive me for this, if such is necessary!) I emphatically insist that leaders who are unwilling to care for their pastors and support their people when they fall into the clutches of injustice are not worthy of ecclesiastical positions and are not even to be mentioned as such in this narrative. May these words serve as a moral challenge to the current leaders of the church; other places and different circumstances may come on the stage of church history, but the principle is the same.

Places and names

Cities, towns, hospitals, and the prison mentioned in this book, as well as the names of departmental organizations, have been altered to avoid identification and further persecution of those who still suffer for their faith in those places. The indicated protagonist of these stories may well be named Benigno, José, Juan, René, Pedro, or Humberto. Real names do not matter; my only purpose is to give glory to God and to offer recognition to all the faithful pastors and laypeople under cruel oppression that have suffered or continue to suffer. There were many of us who were violently persecuted; who can say how many more are to be tested in the bowels of bloody prisons, from East to West?

Chapter 1

Historical Background

So teach us to number our days, that we may gain a heart of wisdom.
—Psalm 90:12

Reopening one's personal book of memories can be fascinating but also excruciatingly painful. There are chapters of my life story that I would prefer never to have lived through and others that would be serenely comforting to forget, but neither of these options is open to me, short of mental senility or my demise. My particular circumstances are destined to pursue me relentlessly during the rest of my earthly days, so I must deal with and learn from them in order to become a better person. Just as steel is forged under intense heat and gold is refined in a furnace, the character is purified in the midst of trials and difficulties. So, like it or not, what each of us has borne in our past through God's mysterious providence makes us the people we are today, with all the warts as well as the accrued virtues. Thank God for this, because in His love and wisdom, He accompanies us along life's path in order to be able to bring forth positive results. Though difficult in the extreme and darkly mysterious as my early experience was, the balance is one that stirs in me deep feelings of gratitude and praise. I hope that after reading this book, you will feel inspired and filled with hope. I also desire for your eyes to be open to not just behold the unfolding drama in these pages but more importantly to make wise decisions about your life and the life of your community.

Fifty years in the history of a people might merit only a brief paragraph in textbooks, but in the life of a single individual, that span of years covers the bulk of one's story. With this in mind, I ask you to pray with me: "So teach us to number our days, that we may gain a heart of wisdom" (Psalm 90:12). Let me tell you a little about my people. I was born into a Christian family of Spanish descent on the west side of the beautiful island of Cuba, the sad land that has fallen from the depths into an even greater abyss. My homeland was once a colony of Spain; then a protectorate of the "Colossus of the North," with frustrated aspirations of attaining full sovereignty; always suffering under misgovernment or oligarchs; and eventually enslaved by its own unnatural children.

This is where I struggled through childhood and my early youth. Those were hard times—very difficult, for certain! And so it has remained, suspended in time, sadly hanging there in space since my earliest memories began. I remember only vaguely the euphoria that swept the island after January 1, 1959, the so-called Triumph of the Revolution. I was still a very young child at that time, but I clearly remember the sense of unfolding history, followed by a growing concern and frustration among the people in the ensuing years as they watched their cherished expectations for progress go south. Along with their vanished freedom went their businesses, bread and milk for their children, and their most basic rights of self-determination.

We were trapped in a lie and forced to live in it, and when the truth appeared, we lamented that the world was sinking . . . as though the collapse of our accustomed world was of little importance as long as we continued on in the lie.

As you read these paragraphs, please understand that I am not motivated by any exacerbated political passion nor inspired by old grudges. I am fundamentally a religious person, and my passion is focused on spiritual matters. So in penning these thoughts, I am pondering the moral rather than the physical well-being and the respect due to the human being. But above all else, I am thinking about the fate of people, including the opposition as well as the defenders of this regime that causes so much misery. If only they could repent, change course, and receive opportune mercy to avoid the fiery indignation of the Righteous Judge who will consume His adversaries on the day of judgment. As far as possible, I will try to curb my personal feelings and limit these comments to real events—historical, proven, and persisting right up to the present—as I compose this chapter, which I do on March 18, 2016. As of this date, after fifty-seven years and seventy-eight days of an imposed administration, no real elections have yet been carried out, no positive changes have been made, and no options for change are yet forthcoming. Invariably, this government represses, imprisons, and kills anyone who dares to raise his voice. At this very moment, as I write, there is another person nearing death after several weeks on a hunger strike, and others are lined up to take his place. These people are willing to give their lives as sacrifices to try to secure the release of at least a few prisoners of conscience who are very ill inside Cuban prisons. I just saw the news on the television, and I suffered the painful images of brave women dressed in white being pushed and beaten because they were interceding for this same cause. They silently bear the blows as they protest against the confinement and inhumane treatment of many worthy prisoners, who literally die in obscurity and darkness in their cells without the national and international communities' willingness to act conscientiously and energetically in their favor. Most people prefer to believe the tale that things are improving. Until now, we've only seen timid actions, isolated and intermittent in this regard.

How much longer and by what legitimate justification must these victims of oppression remain imprisoned simply because they differ from the official ideology of the government? How long will their punishment and slavery go on?

When will there be freedom of speech? When will all Cuban citizens have free access to information from the free world through radio and television, including the Internet, Facebook, Twitter, and any other existing social media? Right now, only a few privileged government employees have limited access to some of it, in spite of all the benefits and concessions that the recent changes in diplomatic relations with the current United States government have brought forth. Some people believe there is a real change in Cuba, but to give the people some inkling of what they deserve is not freedom!

When will the Cuban government stop trying to read even the most intimate thoughts of people to interpret their intentions in order to then judge and imprison them for that? How long will the nations of the world and the world's citizens continue to believe the lies and misrepresentations about the supposed liberty that the Cuban people enjoy? In the meantime, my people are dying.

We pray, God, extend Your merciful arm, as You did when You liberated the Hebrew people from slavery. May all the nations see that there is a God in heaven who still rules the universe—a God who has the authority to raise up and remove kings! Oh, God, as in the past, open up this impossible sea, which yet remains red!

Chapter 2

My Arrival in Hell

*Though I walk through the valley of the shadow of death,
I will fear no evil; for You are with me.*

—Psalm 23:4

When those enormous doors slammed behind me, I got the impression of having entered a hostile and alien world; it struck me that I was being dragged down into the very bowels of hell, and that is exactly what it was! The following weeks would be silent witnesses to the most agonizing and challenging experiences of my young life. I confess that I had never shared with my wife or my children many of the details revealed here; they learned of these facts for the first time when they read this book in the Spanish published version. I never wanted to burden them with or expose them to the shocking aspects of my experience. Throughout the years, this protective husband and father deemed it best to spare them from unnecessary revelations and revulsions.

The guards made me stand in line with about twenty other prisoners, obviously newcomers also; and as commanded by the guards, we began a kind of process of registration where we were assigned our numbers. Next they ordered us to strip down to our underwear and remove our shoes. We were then herded into a rustic barbershop, where we said Goodbye to every hair on our heads. I noticed that they provided no drop cloths, as barbers usually do when cutting hair, but instead they intentionally let the hair fall directly on our bodies. Several complained, but I tried to overlook this minor annoyance, thinking that soon I would be able to shower to get rid of the itchy hairs that were stuck all over my sweaty body. I had no idea at that point just how long it would be until an opportunity would come to take a shower once again.

In our group, there were two ministers, and all the others were individuals convicted of common crimes; soon we ministers began to notice that our treatment was going to be different from theirs. All ordinary prisoners were given blue uniforms and high-top shoes, but we were left standing in our shorts and nothing more. An officer led us into a rough-looking room known as the Office of Reeducation. The official in charge received us with a seemingly friendly smile on his face. Later we learned that the prisoners had a nickname for him—Pistol-Packing Papa—because it was his invariable custom that whenever he entered the cellblocks or when he met an inmate in his office, he always kept his right hand on the butt of his .45-caliber revolver, and if a prisoner spoke back to him he would sneer, "Careful, boy, careful!"

With a cynical demeanor supported by an attitude of unparalleled impudence, this individual launched into an intimidating spiel, all the while obligating us humiliated pastors to stand there in just our briefs and maintain the ridiculous position of staying at attention. That ludicrous image has stuck indelibly in my memory. In other circumstances, I would have died of laughter at such a stupid and brutish sight. The officer seemed like a character pulled out of a crudely written skit by a Karl Marx fanatic, with the skit to be played out at the oddest hour of the night and featuring a sinister buffoon trained to spout mindless political drivel: "Religion is the opium of the people, and you ministers of religion are instruments of imperialism. But the revolution is good, and it has put me here as a comrade trained to teach you to abandon the vices of capitalism, how to change and become new men, useful men, to our new socialist society."

There he paused as if waiting for rapturous applause, but only silence followed. Next he urged us to accept a prepared "voluntary rehabilitation plan." It was the track smart men in our situation opted for; there would be far less *unpleasantness* to deal with as we paid our debt to society in a more *comfortable* section of the prison and with added *benefits* that otherwise we would not receive until we reached a certain level in the reeducation process. He went on to explain what was expected of us if we chose this intelligent path forward:

1. Send a letter of resignation from our former pastorate addressed to the church conference with signed copies for the Ministry of the Interior and the prison management.
2. Attend the prison "study circle" voluntarily, which was nothing more than a kind of indoctrination by which the officers tried to accomplish brainwashing. (It had a lot of success on the weak-minded and cowardly.)
3. Be willing to analyze our past beliefs from the Marxist point of view, and learn to follow the new, improved way. (The reeducator recognized that this process would naturally take some time, but we would have plenty of that.)
4. Accept that the Bible is just a collection of legends and fables, a kind of mythological literature.
5. Set a goal of becoming a new man, useful to socialist society, and so forth.

If all went according to plan, once we had completed our sentences and left prison, the government would give us every opportunity to attend college and study for new careers so that we might launch new lives, working happily to build the greater socialist society, which eventually would lead to the paradise of the proletariat. The final goal was Communism! What splendid enjoyment we would all have in our highly industrialized nation, just like the Soviet Union (such irony!). There would be a great abundance of everything, and this would be equally distributed among all—a society without discrimination, without slaves or masters, without Caesar, without the bourgeoisie, and most important, without a pie-in-the-sky God!

Following his disagreeable discourse, the reeducation man gave us a sheet of paper where we should indicate our acceptance of the rehabilitation plan. Almost in a fatherly tone, he coaxed us: "My sons, accept this offer. I know what I'm talking about. If you refuse, it can become very painful. I assure you that you will regret it if you don't sign. Horrible things happen, especially in section 4. All the inmates are terrified of that area, which they call the 'Lion's den.' It is a very difficult place to survive, and it is impossible to avoid being beaten and even raped by depraved criminals just waiting for the arrival of new prisoners—'fresh meat' they call you—and if you resist them, it could cost you your life. So don't be fools, accept this plan!"

Because our decisions were to be personal, he separated the two of us. This worried me a lot because the other minister was my best friend, someone I loved as a brother. We had been classmates at Colegio Adventista de las Antillas (Antillian College), sang in duets and quartets together, and played the violin and clarinet together in evangelistic meetings and youth congresses. After graduation, we worked in the same conference. There is nothing better than two pastor friends to help each other in difficult times, but we were forced to make this decision alone. I, for my part, had nothing to retract; my fate was sealed. I trusted my friend to remain firm as well—true to God "though the heavens fall."[1]

After a full hour, which felt like a century, the reeducator, Lieutenant Manuel, returned with a devilish grin on his face. How can one ever forget that moment? He told me that my partner had already signed, and he hoped I was as smart as him. I did not answer a word; the sheet of paper remained blank. How could anyone in his right mind believe a word of what this man said? That bald-faced Bolshevik liar surely was trying to manipulate me psychologically with this whole monstrous fabrication. Still, it became disconcerting when my colleague and I were not reunited.

I did not see my friend again for several months and then only a few brief encounters during the entire time we were in prison. Once we found ourselves together in one of those indoctrination sessions that I attended only when forced to do so. But my friend would barely look my way, and he spoke not a word. It was very sad and embarrassing for both of us, I am certain.

One day the theme of a session was evolution versus creation. And the reeducator as well as the instructors thought I would be easy prey, but that was not to be the case. God visited me, and the discussion turned passionate and interesting. I felt that the Lord put His words of wisdom in my mouth, allowing the Bible to defend true science and overcome their materialism. They were demoralized. I was not allowed to speak after that, and they did not make me attend further sessions.

The reeducator's voice, now with a much-less paternal tone, yanked me out of my state of shock: "I'll give you ten minutes to reconsider!" I put on my bravest face and shot back that I didn't need even a minute more. I told him that I did not believe a word of what he said about Pastor H. "He is a good man and faithful to his principles." Lieutenant Manuel laughed in my face and acidly replied, "There are no other principles besides our revolutionary ones, and your religious buddy has totally caved. *Ha, ha, ha.*" This hurt me deeply, but still I answered him with firmness: "If my partner gave in, that is his personal decision; but with God's help, I never will!"

"We'll see about that," he replied.

I practically shouted in his face: "If the other pastor gave in, you better not put much stock in that because nothing good comes from what cowards or traitors do. There are people who have their price and sell themselves to the highest bidder; but there are other men who will not be bought or sold, men who stand firm to the principles of God's Word as truly as the needle to the pole. I am one of those! I believe in God as Creator of the universe, and I believe the Holy Bible is the inspired Word. I believe in Jesus, who was handed over to sinners to be crucified. He died for me! And now, God help me! I have nothing more to add."

The political commissar stood there beside Lieutenant Manuel, listening to my declaration of faith; now the two of them retorted in unison: "Off with him to section 4!" At that time, I did not understand for certain the full significance of that, but soon it was to become frightfully clear. I was assigned to the famous section 4, known as the Lion's den. (You will learn more about this shortly.)

Next they took me to the dressing room, where I put on the blue uniform, but I wasn't so much concerned about that insult to my innocence as I was inwardly grieving for my friend and colleague who had crumpled in the face of fear. I prayed that God would help him get back on track and recover at once from his failure. Sadly, however, that did not happen. I do not want to reveal anything about his identity out of respect for his dear family who meant so much to me. I only relate this episode because it was one of the most painful wounds I suffered that day; it is always hard to see betrayal to God and to His family, which is the church. Hopefully, many can learn a useful lesson from hearing of this shame.

There are people who cower and abandon the path of righteousness when trials and afflictions appear. How unfortunate that is and discouraging to others. It is necessary to face down cowardice! Men and women of principle must remain steadfast in their loyalty to God, even unto death; for only in this way will they receive the crown of life. We must hold steady and not become weak even when we see certain ones from whom we expected much dissolve completely. We must hold on all the tighter to the Savior's hand when those we once had face-to-face communion with now turn their glance away and cannot look us in the eye. It is no easy thing to lose that trust and mutual support from someone who was once our closest of friends; nevertheless, we dare not utterly lose heart.

We can draw value from the cowardice of others and strength out of the weakness of those who abandon the fight. Their coldness can spur our heat. Of course, it's easier to talk about than actually carry off. I learned tough lessons from dealing with cowards: they hide behind anyone, no matter which innocent ones become their unwitting shields. They are capable of sheltering behind a group of children while they take their potshots or from within the walls of a nursing home, no matter the collateral damage of their actions. They think they can avoid pain for themselves or personal loss by simply fleeing the scene when hard reality raises its ugly head.

Many will say, "Poor little cowards, they are that way because fear has them in its grip." But cowardly people dominated by fear can become very dangerous, because out of fear people are capable of the vilest actions: they can deny God, and they can betray their own family or their closest friends. Cowards will die at their own hands before they can be killed. The Bible says that cowards will not enter the kingdom of heaven. During all the time I spent in a Communist prison, following my baptism of fire, I always prayed, "Lord, give me Your courage to overcome. Deliver me from the devil of cowardice even when I stand at the very gates of death and the grave! May the breath from Your Word sustain me and the light of Your lamp illuminate my path." How wonderfully did all the passages of the Bible, which I memorized as a child in my home with my mother and my sisters, strengthen me! The same was true of the verses and chapters I devoured while studying Bible doctrines at the seminary under the direction of Pastor Isaiah de la Torre y Castellón and Pastor Virgilio Zaldívar Marrero. Because there, in prison, I came face-to-face with life. I didn't have a Bible within reach; my family was not there, nor were my brothers in the faith; and my friend had abandoned me and left me in the lurch. So my only resources were prayer and meditation on the Bible passages that I had stored up in better days. The Word was a lamp unto my feet and a light along the dark path that I now had to tread (see Psalm 119:105).

If I have a word of wisdom to share with you personally, dear reader, it is this: read the Bible daily. In this Book, there is a source of unlimited power that can help us live decently during life's normal days, but oh, what a source of tremendous refuge it can be when the evil days begin to rage!

---

1. Ellen G. White, *Education* (Nampa, ID: Pacific Press® Publishing Association, 2002), 57.

Chapter 3

I Tried to Bear It, but I Couldn't

Then I said, "I will not make mention of Him,
nor speak anymore in His name." But His word was in my heart
like a burning fire shut up in my bones;
I was weary of holding it back, and I could not.
—Jeremiah 20:9

The raspy, high-pitched voice of the depraved hall guard in section 4 matched the metallic screech of the heavy barred door leading into the Lion's den: "Fresh meat!" he squealed. Then the insides of that horrendous cave where the dregs of socialist society abide let out a raucous roar followed by sickening applause. I had just turned twenty-two years old, and here I was, living these cruel moments. It all seemed too unreal to be actually happening. How could I possibly be going through this? Was it true, or would I shortly awaken from this filthy nightmare? The perverse voice of the guard, known simply as "Hall" (for the hallway he patrolled), rattled me out of my sense of denial: "Fresh meat!" he trumpeted again, ingratiating himself with the horde of convicted prisoners. A chilling sensation ran down my spine. So then, the scare-inducing spiel of the reeducator was not made up! Everything was happening so fast; it was like bouncing from one rocky ledge to another, ever deeper into the abyss. My racing brain prayed disjointedly, *Lord, don't let go of my hand!* But then came an unexpected force from within, inspired by passages from Nehemiah tucked inside me. A loud voice boomed out of me that silenced everyone: "Lord God of hosts, on the great day, the day of Your second coming, the day of final judgment, don't let this vile scoundrel escape punishment!" The impact this produced was astounding; then the Spirit made me say things I had not forethought or expected to hear trumpet out of my mouth. They were powerful words more or less like these: "Lord, Lord God Almighty in battle! Here is Your servant, tormented like the prophets of old. Bare Your arm before these perverse men, and do not leave me for a moment. Today I ask this of

You: pour the seven last plagues on him who dares touch me!" (Such a daring imprecation.)

I weighed 120 pounds and was not very tall in stature; I always had a strong voice, but that voice coming through me originated beyond my frame. Even as it was happening, I felt it was not just my lung-power or voice; the energy was overwhelming, and it resonated throughout the entire Lion's den! I firmly believe that the invisible presence of the Almighty created a protective shield around me and produced a silencing shock on everyone in that mob, including Hall. He opened my cell door quickly, locked it, and hurried away as though his inner demon was spooked. It goes without saying that by the grace of God no one dared to touch me, not even to threaten me, the whole time I was there.

The welcome cell

The cell measured approximately fourteen feet by ten feet, "plated," in the jargon of the prisoners, which meant that the door was covered with a steel plate and had a small slot at ground level, just big enough to pass an aluminum camp dish and a tin can for water and the watery milk they gave us for breakfast. The menu was invariably a slice of bread about the thickness of my little finger and a serving of Russian powdered milk thinned in water, which had a not-too-unpleasant flavor; but of course, there was never more than half a tin can. The other two meals were equally frugal, enough rice to fill a small matchbox. With so much time on their hands, some prisoners were curious enough to count the grains of rice before eating; it never surpassed 150—that was the record. There was a stew or bean soup, perhaps half a medium ladle's worth, and sometimes if you were lucky, you got a small chunk of squash in your soup.

These minimal meals resulted in bets among prisoners; they played any imaginable game to win a portion of food from a fellow cellmate. For example, you won if a fly (and there were many flies) landed first on your right arm rather than your left arm or such nonsense of that sort. It ended in arguments and fights over the skimpy servings, all in an effort to increase the amount. I couldn't help but think of Cain and Abel in those unequal conflicts and their outcome.

The light we received came from a 25-watt bulb hanging over the center of the cell. Many days would pass before we were moved to an open-barred cell like the other prisoners had rather than a steel-plated door. Then we would also be allowed to go outside for a brief time in the sunlight, though it was always a dangerous experience. For sleeping, there was one double bunk—just that one filthy bunk for all twenty-one men crammed into the cell! Did I say *men*? No, they were hardly humans any longer! No, no, their condition had become worse than beasts.

It gave me considerable pain to see how the enemy had succeeded in destroying the image of the Creator in these persons who, after all, were children of

God. They sometimes fought to a bloody outcome just for a spot on the bunk. Often when a man was asleep, he would be tossed on the floor by others; I remember the horrible sound of their heads striking the floor like coconuts. But if you think I have told you the worst, you would be very wrong. As the days went by, the situation became more and more wretched. Can you imagine twenty-one men having to relieve themselves in a hole four inches in diameter in a corner of the cell? When I arrived in this cell, I was number fifteen, but soon afterward we reached a full house at twenty-one. I never tried sleeping on those filthy bunks. I spent day and night leaning against the wall, sort of slouching down; we could not sit or lie down on the floor because there was urine and feces everywhere. The pain in my legs and back was constant; my feet were swollen and began to putrefy within the wet and infected boots I was wearing. During several days, I was no longer able to eat the meager rations, so I gave them to anyone who wanted them. I didn't talk except to answer the occasional question, doing so only in monosyllables.

My real pain

But my real pain was not physical as much as it was spiritual. Understand me when I say that it is very difficult for a man like me to admit this, but I think that being honest and frank about it helps heal the soul. I was broken; I even thought that God had forsaken me. I was desperate and wanted to die. For the first time in my life, I just wanted to cease to exist, but thankfully, this feeling has never come into my mind since then. Believe me, I would not want any of you to have to go through anything even remotely similar. My life seemed to have ended in complete failure; all my youthful dreams of being a successful preacher—of becoming a renowned evangelist, a pastor beloved by my congregation and the community—had been reduced to a foul-smelling cell full of criminals and waste. I imagined Lucifer and the fallen angels dancing around me with glee at my failure. I was ashamed to think of my wife and my first child soon to be born. What kind of legacy would I leave them?

When I began to pray, I only laid my woeful reproaches on God and then I felt ashamed. I remember saying to Him, "You have deceived me! Are You any better than these Communists? I gave my life to serve You as a minister; while still a child, I became Yours. My youth was placed in Your hands, yet look where You have dumped me. You tricked me! Look what You have done to me; I look like a beggar. If my mother could see me, she would be completely horrified; Celita, my wife, would die of anguish! Enough Lord, I've hit bottom. I want to be done with my life, even if it is a shameful end. I have no more strength to bear this; don't let it go on any longer!"

I tried to bear it, but I couldn't

This seemingly irrational dialogue with my God jarred me to my depths and made me see the true reality of my inner person. Then I asked God what He wanted from me. In saying this, my mind began to receive scenes from the life of the prophet Jeremiah, and I started perceiving that ancient character in the light of my present condition. Although I had no Bible at hand, its passages began flowing with extraordinary clarity.

I saw Jeremiah when he encountered the Word of God and how much joy he felt when he accepted it.

> Your words were found, and I ate them,
> And Your word was to me the joy and rejoicing of my heart;
> For I am called by Your name,
> O Lord God of hosts (Jeremiah 15:16).

This passage brought to my mind the days when I accepted the call to become a minister. Those were challenging but happy days. From the moment I was born, I had been destined to study medicine; it had always been my father's cherished vision for me to be a doctor like my cousins Richard, Bebé, and Cachita. My sisters were nurses. So when I told my father that God had called me to be a minister of the gospel, he put up resistance. He was a good Christian, but he was not willing to compromise. He said, "Our plans for you have always been something other than that. Look how well the doctors in our family live; they all have money! Compare them with the pastors that we know—good people for sure—but they practically die of starvation; they have nothing!"

I replied firmly to my dear father, "I'm sorry that I cannot continue with the family's plans for me; I'm truly sorry I can't please you in this. But God's call is stronger than I can or wish to resist. I shall become a minister. It is a privilege that the Lord has chosen me for the most important calling in the whole world. I am full of joy!"

Then, in the midst of the awfulness of that cell, I wondered if maybe my father had been right. It came to my mind how the prophet Jeremiah, when fulfilling his mission, was unjustly beaten and put in the stocks. That was a cruel and embarrassing punishment, especially when he was put on public display in front of the main door leading into the temple where everyone could mock him (Jeremiah 20:2) There are punishments, and then there are *punishments*! Right?

I beheld the man when he suffered by a conspiracy of betrayal and slander at the hands of those who should have been his friends and brothers: "Come and let us devise plans against Jeremiah" (Jeremiah 18:18). Have you ever had to suffer slander or defamation? How difficult it is! It is especially difficult when slander is loaded upon the back of disgrace; it makes the burden of life four times heavier. I ask myself, *How can God ever forgive slanderers?* But that's one of those incomprehensible things about His love! But I don't want to speak any more on this subject—it's just too ugly and personal. Let me share with you instead the following verses from Rubén Darío, a well-known poet and writer:

Slander

A blob of mud
Upon a diamond can fall,
And in this way
Its brilliance obscure;
But though the diamond entirely
Is found now covered in mire,
It loses not for even an instant
That worth which makes it good
And forever it remains a diamond
No matter the muddy stain!*

I saw this injustice in prison. "And Jeremiah the prophet was shut up in the court of the prison, which was in the king of Judah's house. For Zedekiah king of Judah had shut him up" (Jeremiah 32:2, 3).

I could identify with God's servant when, dejected and discouraged, he tried to withdraw from the prophetic calling; even though I now believe that those accusatory words against the Lord were too strong; but at that moment, they seemed totally appropriate as I spewed them out against my God:

O Lord, You induced me, and I was persuaded;
You are stronger than I, and have prevailed.
I am in derision daily;
Everyone mocks me (Jeremiah 20:7).

In the original language, the meaning is quite raw and can be understood to say, "You seduced me, O Lord." It's like accusing God of deceptively seducing someone through the powers of His divine superiority. That is what the prophet felt, and that is exactly how I felt too. "You called me to something sublime; You taught me one thing, but now You're hitting me with something horribly different. My God, You have betrayed me!"

Jeremiah also said, "I will not make mention of Him, nor speak anymore in His name" (verse 9). I couldn't have said it better than Jeremiah. In other words, "This is as far as I go. Finish this once and for all; send me death! I won't continue being a minister or anything else. It's over!"

---

* Translation of Rubén Darío, "La Calumnia."

This disposition is what made me reach rock bottom. Could I really abandon all that I truly was? Would the devil be allowed to win this battle?

Immediately after Jeremiah said he wanted to give up, he then said he couldn't because of the message he had,

His word is in my heart like a fire,
a fire shut up in my bones.
I am weary of holding it in;
indeed, I cannot (verse 9, NIV).

At that very moment, the filthy and foul-smelling cell was illuminated. I don't remember what time it was, and I can't recall what the other prisoners were doing. I stood up, and my body filled with a heavenly power. I belted out these words, which produced a distinctly supernatural echo:

But the LORD is with me as a mighty, awesome One.
Therefore my persecutors will stumble, and will not prevail.
They will be greatly ashamed, for they will not prosper.
Their everlasting confusion will never be forgotten (verse 11).

From that moment, I could see everything clearly: God had brought me there with a mission—an important mission. There were many people in that place who needed God; there were many souls to save; and this was my new field of labor. This was now my church, my new church, the prison church at 5 Luis Lazo. I needed to cease my laments; I needed to stop feeling sorry for myself; and I needed to get to work right away.

God clearly gave me a plan of action. My mind had been weakened by a state of doubt and rebellion, but now everything changed as though in the blink of an eye. I had recovered my emotional and spiritual balance through the presence and touch of the Holy Spirit. And so I decided that I would never abandon my ministry, no matter what might happen; then I begged God to forgive me for my lack of faith, for my lack of confidence in Him, and for the wrong way I had treated my Lord. From within that filthy pit, I prayed to God, like Jonah in the belly of the fish, and asked for the strength to take my ministry to the end with humility, honor, and dignity.

Immediately, I called out to the hall guard, who was just then approaching our cell to see what was happening. "Hall!" He answered with his shrill voice: "What's going on here?" Then I said, "What's happening here is that God has manifested Himself in this place, and He does not want us to remain in this filthy condition! This cannot go on; we are rotting in this foul mess. What is happening here is that although we are prisoners we are not animals; we need to clean this place up, bathe, and change clothes. If this doesn't happen very soon, there will be an epidemic in this place, which will cost your revolution way too much in doctors' bills and medicine. If you are smart, you'll get us soap and water."

Hall was terrified and visibly shocked by the flash of light, similar to a bolt of lightning, escaping our cell and by the booming voice he heard as well. My cellmates were dumbfounded; each one trying to come up with an explanation for the strange phenomenon. But they were at a loss for words to explain what had just occurred. I had no time to waste explaining it to them; I was now a man with a mission and I must comply. I said to Hall, "If you want, I will explain this later; but right now, you must help us, please, so that we can clean ourselves up." He replied that he could not authorize bathroom privileges for us or open the cell to clean it. "But I'll talk to the sergeant in charge."

I have no idea what he said to the sergeant, but not long after, Sergeant G. himself appeared to inspect the place. He gave orders that we were to be allowed to clean the cell and that two sets of underwear, uniforms, and new boots were to be issued to each one of us. Before leaving, he called me aside and quietly said, "I know who you are, and I know you are a good man. I know your church because my neighbor, Rosa Mezquía [that is her real name; she sleeps in Jesus now], attends your congregation. That woman is the best person I have ever met in my life. She was very good to us during my mother's illness, and just yesterday she told me about you. I'll give orders to help. Starting today, you'll bathe every day, and this cell will be cleaned in regular order just as all the others. And as soon as I can, I'll get you out of here."

I thanked the sergeant and prayed silently for him. May God reward him for what he did for me and for others after me. But in a very special way, God bless the memory of Rosa and her entire family! I will always keep this experience in my heart with gratitude. The selfless Christian service of a member of my church touched Sergeant G.'s life (I will not mention his real name for obvious reasons). He did a wonderful thing for me, and after his secret conversion, he continued aiding the underground church in prison.

A good Christian testimony can touch the heart of anyone, no matter who it is or for whom that person works. Blessings can reach those who least expect them and at the most opportune moment.

Chapter 4

The Torch

And so we have the prophetic word confirmed, which you do well to heed
as a light that shines in a dark place, until the day dawns
and the morning star rises in your hearts.

—2 Peter 1:19

Did you hear that, men? We're going to clean up all this filth and then take showers because later we will have an important meeting," I said in a voice that expressed confidence. We worked for more than two hours, and in the end, our cell was completely transformed. We even got the authorities to bring us a jug of Pinaroma (a pine-scented disinfectant), which made the environment much more tolerable than it had been.

Once everything was clean and tidy, I invited those who were interested to sit in a circle on the floor. "I will tell you about a prisoner whose story is in the Bible." Gradually, all the cellmates joined the circle, at first perhaps because they had nothing better to do. Soon, however, all without exception showed considerable interest. One of the "brothers" (as I began to call them intentionally) from the new "church," who we'll call Gravarán, spoke up with a slight hint of wryness: "How is it possible that in the Bible, a book that only speaks about the lives of the saints, there is a story about a convicted prisoner like me?"

"Good question, Brother," I replied. "Even though I don't have a Bible in my hands, let me tell you first what the Bible is and what it says about itself." And I continued to explain: "The Bible is God's revelation to humans; it is made up of sixty-six books bound in a single volume. Twenty-two of those books are mainly historical, eighteen are largely prophetic, there are twenty-one letters, and there are five primarily poetic books. The Holy Scriptures, as we also call the Bible, contain true stories about the lives of real people. Many did very good and wonderful things, while others did really wicked things. If the Bible only told about good things done by saintly people, that would hardly be true to life, and few would consider it reliable. It is plain to see that no human being is perfect, only God is perfect. So, when we consider human lives, we must take into account both the positive and the negative aspects.

"Although the Bible was written by at least thirty-six authors—some were kings, farmers, generals, fishermen, ministers, and priests; one was a doctor, another a tax collector; some poor, and others rich—and although the writing of the Bible took about sixteen hundred years, it is nevertheless still one unified Book because God is its Author."

"How can that be possible?" Alejandro asked dubiously. He was a gray-haired man who, in his earlier years, had been a professor of literature at a high school, but now he was serving a double sentence on charges of ideological "diversion" and homosexual practices.

"Brother Alejandro, this exceptional unity of thought was only possible in such a grand work as the Bible through the intervention of the Spirit of God, who inspired each one of those authors. None of them simply wrote whatever popped into their heads: 'For prophecy never came by the will of man, but holy men of God spoke as they were moved by the Holy Spirit' " (2 Peter 1:21).

"Do you mean to say that the Holy Spirit dictated word for word to these authors that wrote the Bible?" he asked again, showing his keen interest.

"Let me help you understand this point correctly," I replied, "because it is good to get things right from the start: God gave the prophets and writers revelations and dreams, and they took the clear concepts given to them by the will of God and wrote down what was inspired using their own words and language skills. The Holy Spirit also helped the writers to express the thoughts clearly so that the divine message would be communicated correctly. The task of the Bible writers was tremendous; it was their great responsibility to speak in the name of the Creator of the universe. We can summarize the process by saying that 'the Holy Spirit revealed to the prophets what God wanted them to know' so that they in turn could communicate the message to the people 'and then guided them in proclamation of that message. Some spoke the word; others wrote it down,'[1] and those writings became what we now know as the Bible.

"Let me mention a few examples: David the prophet and king said, 'The Spirit of the LORD spoke by me, and His word was on my tongue' [2 Samuel 23:2]. The prophet Jeremiah wrote, 'The LORD said to me: "Behold, I have put My words in your mouth" ' " (Jeremiah 1:9).

"So what part of the Bible is inspired?" Alejandro persisted.

I repeated from memory what the apostle Paul wrote to Timothy: "All Scripture is given by inspiration of God, and is profitable for doctrine, for reproof, for correction, for instruction in righteousness, that the man of God may be complete, thoroughly equipped for every good work" (2 Timothy 3:16, 17).

"That's what I need—to be instructed to do good works," said Nicolas, a man of Russian descent who was serving a sentence of thirty-five years for killing, with his bare hands, his mother's lover, who also happened to be his boss at work. He had walked in on them and went into a senseless rage. "If I'd had some religion in my life, maybe I wouldn't be in jail today," he lamented. "But I never even knew if God existed or not; I grew up like a wild animal, learning to defend myself from whoever attacked me and hating everyone who was more powerful than I was. That's what old Slovasevich taught me before being electrocuted. Then, because my angry mother testified against me during the murder trial, I ended up here."

"All that may be true, Brother Nicolas, but God is willing to overlook our times of ignorance and receive us as His beloved children. Memorize this: God is love."

"Love?" Almansa interrupted, who, from what I had observed since entering that cell, was the most cynical of the group. It seemed he had read a lot but learned very little; he was always intent on twisting around what others had to say. "I read a book by the great author Vargas Vila about what love really is," he interjected, and then he quoted a passage that I have never forgotten because of its negativity: "Fear love just as you fear death—it is death itself. By it, we are born, and by it, we die. Be strong, so you can live without it. Love is the Alpha and the Omega; the beginning and the end of existence. It is a curse."[2] Almansa, I learned later, had indeed read that work, and he had an impressive memory.

"So if God is love, I'd rather stay as far away from Him as possible," he declared. Right then, I was ready to refute him, but I perceived that Almansa was a broken man, so I decided to keep silent and listen. "I loved a woman once, I loved her more than myself; but she did not love me in return or respect me," he shared. I wasn't trying to promote a session of life-story anecdotes, but something was motivating that convict to open up his heart, so I decided to listen without interrupting.

"I was a respected member of the Communist Party. Although I had reservations about the system of government, I never expressed them because I was doing well and preferred to go with the flow. I was manager of the Regional Railway Transport Company; had a good house; a car at my disposal, paid by the company; and other benefits; but my dilemma began when the party decided to send me on an international mission to Angola, Africa. [Cuban political operatives, doctors, teachers, soldiers, and others are sent to cooperate with like-minded governments abroad.] Things were not very good there. I was not a soldier but was in charge of training political cadres. Many people there hated Cubans; we were targeted almost daily. The same 'friends' we worked with during the day could become our murderers at night. I heard about some natives eating certain parts of their Cuban victims because they believed doing so would make them brave and victorious like us.

"I was at the point of a nervous breakdown. I could not sleep. I made sure someone tasted my food before I ate it because I thought someone was going to poison me. I lived in constant fear; but I could not get out of the assignment, so I ended up spending almost two years there, during which time I saw my wife only once. Then one day something unexpected happened. I received an official call from Cuba; it was from the provincial party secretary general, who informed me that I was to return to the island immediately. Upon landing at José Martí International Airport, two members from the political bureau were waiting for me. They told me I could not go to my home, instead we must go straight to the offices of the party as the meeting was urgent and important. I asked myself, *What can be the reason for such mystery?* Then the secretary general said very calmly, 'We have confidential information that your wife is being unfaithful to you.' The world under my feet seemed to give way, and I nearly toppled over. The official stated that I must divorce her before flying back to Angola. It wouldn't be acceptable for a party member to continue to be married to an unfaithful woman.

"I was in a state of shock, but then I heard him say something curious that made me wonder what was really going on: 'If you don't divorce your wife immediately, we will have to expel you dishonorably from the party ranks, and that would mean the end of your international assignment.' So I thought to myself, *This is my chance to get out of all my problems at once. If it is true that my wife is cheating on me, why should I continue to stay married to her? But if I tell them that I refuse to divorce her, I'll get out of having to go back to Angola, and I'll be done with the party. This plan can set me free of all my problems at once.* So, pretending to be very offended, I accused them of being perverse slanderers: 'My wife would never do such a thing! You are making up this story based on pure gossip.' And such was my 'anger' that all my comrades were convinced by my performance that I was the suffering, betrayed spouse. The following day I was informed that the sanctions against me included my removal from the party. They took away my party membership card. They told me that although I was allowed to keep my job at the transport company, I would not be able to continue in my administrative post and I would be demoted to an assistant. However, they would respect my regular salary."

"And how was it that you ended up here?" asked the most impatient one of the group. A prolonged silence followed. Almansa sighed deeply, as if not wanting to remember those days, and continued with his story.

"To tell the truth, I felt relieved about not returning to the torture of Angola, and it was fine by me having no further commitment to the party. I figured as soon as prudently feasible, I would divorce my cheating wife. She and I continued living in the same house, and it was an ordeal just to see her, but that was something I had to put up with for the time being. I never had intimate relations with my wife again. Although she denied ever cheating, it was clear she was not at all interested in saving our marriage. According to her, it was all my fault that our love had died because I had accepted that long mission to Angola.

So after waiting four months, I went ahead and initiated the divorce. Things were apparently going well for me for the first time in a long time—until someone brought me news that stirred up the very devil in me.

"Yes, it was true. My wife had been having an affair with another man! They had been involved for a long time, even before my mission to Angola, and I had not known about it. But the hardest part, which now explained everything clearly, was that the other man was none other than the secretary general of the party. I was also informed of the place where they had their trysts and of the approximate time. My pride and self-worth were wounded; filled with rage, I began planning revenge. I still had the gun assigned to me in Angola, as nobody had ordered me to return it. Infuriated, I was capable of anything. I went to the place where they normally met; I found them together and riddled them with bullets. On the day of the trial, I was sentenced to thirty years imprisonment for the crime of premeditated murder and malice aforethought. But what I regret the most is that in my anger I wasted all the bullets on them and didn't leave one for my own head. It would have all been over for me in an instant. But here I am now, shattered! It feels like I have a rat chewing on my innards here in this place. I live trying to forget, but I can't. They were to blame! Only them. They mocked me! So, Mr. Preacher, don't talk to me about love."

How easy it is to judge people by their appearances. There before me was a man who from the beginning I had judged harshly; *the most cynical of the group*, I had said to myself. He was tensed up, with clenched teeth and tight fists, but now it was clear from the expression on his face that he was nothing more than a victim, a human being who needed help. I could never justify his actions, as crime is never justifiable. But this convict was just another prisoner of Satan, who enjoys taking people who, under other circumstances, might have been good people and even blessings to their fellow human beings and incites them to commit appalling actions that will weigh upon them for the rest of their lives.

At that moment, I felt full of compassion. I was beginning to have a better understanding of God's purpose in allowing me to fall into that pit. There was a work to do, though at that time I only had a glimpse of what might be accomplished. I still had no idea of all the great things that God wanted to do in that place on behalf of those poor souls. I prayed silently. God heard my prayer, and I felt that my best pastoral skills were about to unfold.

Right then the words began to flow, not from my lips but from deep inside, and I called that murderer my brother. But I did not do so as a mere strategy to bring about change in the men of that cell, I called him "Brother" from my heart because I knew he was a child of God, just like me. Someone who, in the midst of his violent experience and suffering, was crying out for help. I was not wrong about that because when he heard my words—not really *my* words, but a mixture of biblical texts stored in my memory and my thoughts from a revered writer who impacted my training since childhood—he began to nod in agreement and a remarkable change came over his countenance.

"Brother Almansa, and brothers all, the true meaning of love is not subject to the philosophical or poetic interpretation of any writer caught up in unstable musings and uncommitted to the foundations of truth and human dignity, such as in the case of José María Vargas Vila, the writer you mentioned. It is not my intention to judge his literary work, which is very controversial to be sure, or his intentions; I just want to reject his concepts in this erroneous interpretation of love. We're not talking about the common love found in the basic physical attraction that can exist between two human beings and not about whimsical love as a passion in pursuit of its own pleasure. No, we are not describing a weak little feeling of love that only seeks its selfish desires. Do you want to know what love truly is?"

"Yes," several of them said aloud, and others nodded their heads affirmatively.

I then spoke to them with strong inspiration: " 'Love is patient, love is kind. It does not envy, it does not boast, it is not proud. It does not dishonor others, it is not self-seeking, it is not easily angered, it keeps no record of wrongs. Love does not delight in evil but rejoices in truth. It always protects, always trusts, always hopes, always perseveres. Love never fails. But where there are prophecies, they will cease; where there are tongues, they will be stilled; where there is knowledge, it will pass away' (1 Corinthians 13:4–8). The love I am referring to when I talk about God is not the erotic love that can exist between a man and a woman; it is not even filial love between siblings and relatives. What I am referring to is divine *agape*, which is the most sublime expression of love because it is the very essence of the Supreme Being. It is the most perfect description of the Creator of the universe. The Bible says that God is love, not merely that He feels love or knows love. 'And we have known and believed the love that God has for us. God is love, and he who abides in love abides in God, and God in him' " (1 John 4:16).

"Brothers," Máximo (a Freemason) interjected, "I'd like to explain that God the Creator is the Divine Architect of the universe, right?"

"Well said, Brother Max, God is the Designer and Maker of everything we see in nature! In fact, nature is God's second book; it is what theologians call natural revelation:

"Nature and revelation alike testify of God's love. Our Father in heaven is the source of life, of wisdom, and of joy. Look at the wonderful and beautiful things of nature. Think of their marvelous adaptation to the needs and happiness, not only of man, but of all living creatures. The sunshine and the rain, that gladden and refresh the earth, the hills and seas and plains, all speak to us of the Creator's love. It is God who supplies the daily needs of all His creatures. . . .

" 'God is love' is written upon every opening bud, upon every spire of springing grass. The lovely birds making the air vocal with their happy songs, the delicately tinted flowers in their perfection perfuming the air, the lofty trees of the forest with their rich foliage of living green—all testify to the tender, fatherly care of our God and to His desire to make His children happy."[3]

"You have more words than Vargas Vila!" exclaimed Almansa, who I previously considered a cynic. This was the first praise I heard in prison. I countered, "I'm not sure about that. I know I don't have much in common with him. But the words that I am sharing with you are not mine, they are part of the inspired Word of God. My part is to study it and then to teach it to others."

"So then, you are a teacher of religion?" Brother Nicolas asked.

I smiled and replied, "Well, yes, something like that." I went on to explain to them what pastors are and what they are dedicated to do in their ministry. Ever since then, everyone started calling me "Teacher."

---

1. Gerhard Pfandl, "Revelation-Inspiration," *Adult Sabbath School Bible Study Guide*, devotional for January 25, 2009, accessed September 7, 2016, https://absg.adventist.org/assets/public/files/lessons/2009/1Q/SE/PDFs/EAQ109_05.pdf.

2. Translated from José María Vargas Vila, *Ibis* (Paris: Librería Americana, 1917), 21.

3. Ellen G. White, *Steps to Christ* (Washington, DC: Review and Herald® Publishing Association, 1956), 9, 10.

Chapter 5

What Do Those Who Have Not Suffered Know About Life?

"Look, this dreamer is coming!"

—Genesis 37:19

I felt admired and respected by the other prisoners and grateful to God, but not because they called me teacher or because I felt safer in the midst of that dangerous and sinister place. I was grateful because I had just started my ministry in prison and already the Spirit was working powerfully for the good of that group.

It is necessary for every human being to experience some degree of self-esteem, which for obvious reasons is rarely present in the lives of convicts, especially those serving sentences for bloody deeds, robbery, and a whole range of crimes and common delinquencies. It is very common to find among prisoners, at least in my experience, people who are so hardened and so calloused in their consciences that they do not seem to feel anguish about their condition, nor do they have any concern for the pain of others. But that is only by appearance.

The often-heard and quasi-philosophical expression "What do those who have not suffered know about life?" which most of the prisoners repeat, places men such as these on an imaginary plane, making them feel different and even superior to other mortals. What this comes down to, however, is the rationalization that they do not need to explain themselves or their situations: I don't have to explain anything to you. You are not qualified to understand! But in reality, this is just a way to evade facing the reality of mistakes committed. This phrase can be real, but only in the environment of a prison subculture. We need to take into account the fact that people don't rise above their failures without first hitting bottom, rebounding, and then determining to get back up to the surface and start new lives. I knew the first thing these men needed was to understand the meaning of acceptance: they needed to accept their condition, to accept reality, to accept the world around them, and to know that God was willing to accept them too, just as they were. Often the consciousness of guilt clouds understanding and does not allow sinners, afflicted by their wickedness, to accept that there is forgiveness as well as a way back to the *good*.

Those prisoners as well as the other inmates of section 4, with whom we lived, were nothing more than a group of human beings—who were also children of the heavenly Father—who had been victims. Of course, victims of the consequences of their own faults or perhaps of their diverse circumstances, but definitely victims of the enemy of the Creator, who tries to erase the image and likeness of God from every person. Satan's specialty is to take hold of God's children and turn them into monsters. But Jesus Christ's specialty is to take those monsters and transform them into God's beloved sons and daughters.

I sensed it was the right time to introduce one of the great heroes of Scripture, from whom they would receive the inspiration that I myself received. I wanted them to know about that prisoner, whose example could be a moral boost for them and help them to think in a nobler and uplifting way, perhaps for the first time in their lives.

I decided to take up again the story I had first shared with them about the biblical prisoner. Clearly, the Holy Spirit had used it in a powerful way as a starting point of approach. Most certainly there was common ground between Joseph, the son of Jacob, when he was imprisoned and this group of prisoners. Weren't we all prisoners? I thought it would be wise to go from the known to the unknown. So I told them the story that went something like this: "Far away and long ago in eastern lands, back in the time of the patriarchs, there was a man named Jacob who had twelve sons. Theirs was a rather unique family composed of the patriarch, his two wives, Leah and Rachel, and their two maidservants, Bilhah and Zilpah.

"These were the sons by Leah: Reuben, the firstborn; Simeon, Levi, Judah, Issachar, and Zebulun. The sons by Rachel: Joseph and Benjamin. The sons of Bilhah, Rachel's maidservant: Dan and Naphtali. And the sons of Zilpah, maidservant of Leah: Gad and Asher. The family settled in the land of Canaan, where Jacob's father Isaac had dwelt."

In my own words, I told them the story as it appears in Genesis 27:2–11:

Joseph, being seventeen years old, was feeding the flock with his brothers. And the lad was with the sons of Bilhah and the sons of Zilpah, his father's wives; and Joseph brought a bad report of them to his father.

Now Israel [Jacob] loved Joseph more than all his children, because he was the son of his old age. Also he made him a tunic of many colors. But when his brothers saw that their father loved him more than all his brothers, they hated him and could not speak peaceably to him.

Now Joseph had a dream, and he told it to his brothers; and they hated him even more. So he said to them, "Please hear this dream which I have dreamed: There we were, binding sheaves in the field. Then behold, my sheaf arose and also stood upright; and indeed your sheaves stood all around and bowed down to my sheaf."

And his brothers said to him, "Shall you indeed reign over us? Or shall you indeed have dominion over us?" So they hated him even more for his dreams and for his words.

Then he dreamed still another dream and told it to his brothers, and said, "Look, I have dreamed another dream. And this time, the sun, the moon, and the eleven stars bowed down to me."

So he told it to his father and his brothers; and his father rebuked him and said to him, "What is this dream that you have dreamed? Shall your mother and I and your brothers indeed come to bow down to the earth before you?" And his brothers envied him, but his father kept the matter in mind.

I continued to paraphrase the rest of the chapter (verses 12–36): "After a while, his brothers went to feed their father's flock in a place called Shechem. One day Jacob said to his son Joseph, 'I want you to see how things are going for your brothers and the flock; go find out and bring me word.' So Joseph went to Shechem in the Hebron Valley, but he didn't find his brothers grazing the sheep there. When he asked around for them, he was told that they had gone to a place called Dothan. Joseph traveled on and finally located them.

"But when they saw him coming in the distance, before he got to where they were, they conspired to kill him.

"The brothers said among themselves, 'Look, here comes the dreamer. What do you say we kill him and throw his body into a pit? We can later tell Father that some wild beast must have devoured him; then we shall see what becomes of his dreams.'

"But the oldest brother, Reuben, persuaded them not to kill him but instead to toss him into a dry well in the wilderness and leave him there. In reality, Reuben had in mind rescuing Joseph at a later time.

"When Joseph caught up with his brothers, they grabbed him and stripped off his coat of many colors, next they took him and cast him into the cistern; it was empty—there was no water in it.

"The brothers sat down to eat bread, and when they looked up, a company of Ishmaelite merchants appeared on the road, coming from Gilead. Their camels were loaded with spices, balms, and myrrh, which they were taking to Egypt to sell.

"Then Judah said to his brothers, 'What good can come out of killing our brother and concealing his blood? Come on, let's sell him to the Ishmaelites and not bloody our hands; he is our brother, after all.' And his brothers agreed with him.

"When the merchants came close, the brothers pulled Joseph out of the pit and sold him to the Ishmaelites for twenty pieces of silver. Those men took Joseph with them down to Egypt.

"Following that, the brothers took Joseph's coat, killed a kid goat, and dipped the coat in its blood. Later they took the coat of many colors to their father and said, 'We have found this. Do you think it might be your son's coat, or not?'

"Poor old Jacob knew it was Joseph's and said, 'It is my son's. A wild beast has devoured him; Joseph has been torn to pieces.'

"Then Jacob tore his clothes and dressed in sackcloth. He mourned for his son many days. And all his sons and daughters tried to comfort him, but he refused to be comforted and said, 'I will go to my grave mourning for Joseph, my son.' He wept and grieved."

How many cases have we seen of parents who have mourned over the misfortunes that befall their children! Too often the blame is laid entirely on the children for the blunders they commit. But what about the responsibilities of the parents? Many times the children's actions are a repetition of the actions of their parents. The mistakes of the children, at times, are nothing more than a directly proportional reaction to the mistakes of their progenitors.

I said earlier that Jacob's family was a rather unique family: a man who had twelve sons by four women. That might seem amusing to some, but the fruits of wrongdoing are generally not sweet or pleasurable.

> The sin of Jacob, and the train of events to which it led, had not failed to exert an influence for evil—an influence that revealed its bitter fruit in the character and life of his sons. As these sons arrived at manhood they developed serious faults. The results of polygamy were manifest in the household. This terrible evil tends to dry up the very springs of love, and its influence weakens the most sacred ties. The jealousy of the several mothers had embittered the family relation, the children had grown up contentious and impatient of control, and the father's life was darkened with anxiety and grief.[1]

Chapter 37 of the book of Genesis ends with what is the beginning of Joseph's traumatic events and truly amazing experience in Egypt. The last verse announces in few words a monumental misfortune in the life of the young man: "Now the Midianites [Ishmaelites] had sold him in Egypt to Potiphar, an officer of Pharaoh and captain of the guard" (verse 36).

I had chosen the story of Joseph for its great drama and for the lessons that could apply to that group of prisoners. Although I don't remember all my explanations, there are various concepts that even today deeply move me. Allow me to share with my present-day readers part of what I preached in that cell, falling back now on the Bible and *Patriarchs and Prophets*, the wonderful book I've already cited.

Becoming a slave is a fate worse than death. Life is meaningless when there is no freedom. Human beings were created as free beings; we were endowed with the power to make our own decisions.

What happened to Joseph was a huge injustice. Due to the numerical superiority and perhaps the greater physical strength of his own brothers, the young man was overcome, subdued, bound, and physically abused. He was deprived of his liberty undeservingly, and he was sentenced to slavery when he deserved to be free.

God does not approve of the heinous attitudes or of the despicable actions of abusers and enslavers. People acting from positions of physical or numerical superiority, or relying on the power of weapons, in order to forcefully control the lives of other people and deprive them of their rights will have to render their accounts someday before the judgment of humans, before the court of their own consciences, but primarily before the Magistrate of the universe, who cannot be mocked or deceived with false evidence. While God's love is immeasurable, His justice is also unavoidable.

I pause here to direct these words to my present-day readers: If you hold a position of influence and authority, in whatever area that may be—whether in the political, social, or religious environment—I invite you to be just and respectful of other people's freedom. Being just brings tranquility to the soul and peace to human existence, and above all else it makes Heaven smile.

If you are someone who has practiced or practices abuse, please stop while there is still time to make things right! Whether you exercise your violence within your home or from a position of privilege, while there is life, there remains an opportunity for sincere repentance. Do not continue to make decisions for others. Do not encroach on those under your authority in what they do, say, eat, how they dress, or think. It may be that you think you are right in what you do or have done. If your fellow human beings have been deprived of their individual or collective rights, then there can be no doubt about it: your actions have been motivated by an erroneous philosophy or wrong line of thought. Please do not prolong the agony; now is the time to rectify things before it is way too late. For many, your actions may have already reached the limit and sealed the misfortune forever; but for the sake of those who remain, please change. Do not allow your name to be recorded forever as a curse!

Joseph wept bitterly and gave in to pain and despair, as many of us have done in our own situations. Being away from his family, home, and paternal affection was very difficult to bear. "What a change in situation—from the tenderly cherished son to the despised and helpless slave! Alone and friendless, what would be his lot in the strange land to which he was going?"[2] He did not even understand the language of his masters. How piercing was his uncertainty in those dark days!

"But, in the providence of God, even this experience was to be a blessing to him. . . . His father, strong and tender as his love had been, had done him wrong by his partiality and indulgence. . . . Its effects were manifest also in his own character. Faults had been encouraged that were now to be corrected. He was becoming self-sufficient and exacting,"[3] which offended his brothers and perhaps bothered those he associated with. Something that was very beneficial for Joseph in his life was the religious instruction he had received at home. In the midst of his misfortune, he decided to be faithful to the God of his fathers. From a spoiled child, he was transformed into a serene and courageous man.

That sermon on the life of Joseph was the longest sermon of my ministerial life. I talked to the group of prisoners all afternoon and through the night until our breakfast arrived the following morning. I was amazed; it seemed impossible to look at those hardened faces bathed in tears. No one fell asleep; they were all deeply touched. If I remember correctly, it was Gravarán who exclaimed, "I think those same angels who helped Jacob and Joseph were the ones who came right here last night to help you, Teacher, and they are helping all of us as well."

"Of that, you can be sure, Brother Gravarán. They are certainly with us," I replied.

Then I raised a silent prayer for all those present and praised God in my heart: *Thank You, Lord, for what is happening here with these men!* Afterward, I suggested that it was time to conclude; but almost in unison they protested, "Continue! Don't stop now halfway through. We want to know how the story of Joseph ends." So I took a deep breath and launched forth again, as continued in the following chapter.

1. Ellen G. White, *Patriarchs and Prophets* (Nampa, ID: Pacific Press® Publishing Association, 2002), 208.

2. Ibid., 213.

3. Ibid.

Chapter 6

Slavery and Prison

"How then can I do this great wickedness, and sin against God?"
—Genesis 39:9

I now continue with the story of Joseph that I shared with my prison cellmates:

> Now Joseph had been taken down to Egypt. And Potiphar, an officer of Pharaoh, captain of the guard, an Egyptian, bought him from the Ishmaelites who had taken him down there. The LORD was with Joseph, and he was a successful man; and he was in the house of his master the Egyptian. And his master saw that the LORD was with him and that the LORD made all he did to prosper in his hand. So Joseph found favor in his sight, and served him. Then he made him overseer of his house, and all that he had he put under his authority. So it was, from the time that he had made him overseer of his house and all that he had, that the LORD blessed the Egyptian's house for Joseph's sake; and the blessing of the LORD was on all that he had in the house and in the field. Thus he left all that he had in Joseph's hand, and he did not know what he had except for the bread which he ate (Genesis 39:1–6).

Joseph remained in the service of his Egyptian master, Potiphar, for about ten years, during which time he was an honest and respectful young man. The Scriptures say that God prospered him during his time of slavery. No matter the human condition, whoever accepts the Lord and receives Him as Father and Savior, even if that person is a prisoner or a slave, will be considered a child of God, and nobody can deprive him of the blessings the heavenly Father has for him.

"The marked prosperity which attended everything placed under Joseph's care was not the result of a direct miracle; but his industry, care, and energy were crowned with the divine blessing. Joseph attributed his success to the favor of God, and even his idolatrous master accepted this as the secret of his unparalleled prosperity. Without steadfast, well-directed effort, however, success could never have been attained."[1]

No matter the circumstances that you face—whether you're at the head of a prosperous business in the most developed country in the world or imprisoned in a miserable dungeon, a slave in an unknown land or held captive by guerrilla forces in the middle of a jungle—integrity, faith, diligence, and respect for others will produce good results with God's blessing.

"Joseph's gentleness and fidelity won the heart of the chief captain, who came to regard him as a son rather than a slave. The youth was brought in contact with men of rank and learning, and he acquired a knowledge of science, of languages, and of affairs—an education needful to the future prime minister of Egypt."[2]

But let's not get ahead of the story! Things did not flow quite that easily or move along so rapidly. The trials Joseph faced were not simple.

I always say, "Blessed are misfortunes, but only when they come alone!" Generally, problems seem to gang up on us in concerted attacks. That's what happened to Joseph at this point in the story; one of the hardest situations in his life was about to confront him.

> Now Joseph was handsome in form and appearance.
> And it came to pass after these things that his master's wife cast longing eyes on Joseph, and she said, "Lie with me."
> But he refused and said to his master's wife, "Look, my master does not know what is with me in the house, and he has committed all that he has to my hand. There is no one greater in this house than I, nor has he kept back anything from me but you, because you are his wife. How then can I do this great wickedness, and sin against God?" (verses 6–9).

What a complication! As if Joseph's trials hadn't already been enough, now this thorn is added on. Joseph's faith and integrity would be tested in the crucible. His trial by fire was intensifying. Joseph analyzed the difficult situation. He had before him two options. If he succumbed to the seduction, he would have to live a life of concealment and lies from that point on. If he held true to his principles, he would face adversity, imprisonment, and possibly death.

Joseph decided to be faithful. He decided to live as if in the presence of God. He knew that nothing of what we do escapes God's knowledge. In spite of his refusal, his master's wife did not relent in her efforts to make him fall to her temptations. Infatuated by this young slave, she persisted without any results, until one day, when they were alone, she decided to take her obsession to the the next level. The Bible says:

> So it was, as she spoke to Joseph day by day, that he did not heed her, to lie with her or to be with her.

But it happened about this time, when Joseph went into the house to do his work, and none of the men of the house was inside, that she caught him by his garment, saying, "Lie with me." But he left his garment in her hand, and fled and ran outside. And so it was, when she saw that he had left his garment in her hand and fled outside, that she called to the men of her house and spoke to them, saying, "See, he has brought in to us a Hebrew to mock us. He came in to me to lie with me, and I cried out with a loud voice. And it happened, when he heard that I lifted my voice and cried out, that he left his garment with me, and fled and went outside."

So she kept his garment with her until his master came home. Then she spoke to him with words like these, saying, "The Hebrew servant whom you brought to us came in to me to mock me; so it happened, as I lifted my voice and cried out, that he left his garment with me and fled outside."

So it was, when his master heard the words which his wife spoke to him, saying, "Your servant did to me after this manner," that his anger was aroused. Then Joseph's master took him and put him into the prison, a place where the king's prisoners were confined. And he was there in the prison (verses 10–20).

That was how Joseph became a prisoner. Joseph suffered unjustly for being an honorable man. The woman who tempted him, seeing herself rejected, decided to take revenge, accusing Joseph of a horrible sin that he had not committed and causing him to be put in prison.

To be honest, we must accept the fact that Potiphar probably never believed the story he was told; he most likely knew what type of woman his wife was. If he had believed the fabrication, without a doubt, Joseph would have been put to death. But for the sake of saving his family's reputation, and without taking into account the loyalty, the diligence, the modesty, and the integrity that his servant had consistently displayed, Joseph's master abandoned him to disgrace and a life of imprisonment.[3] The psalmist describes Joseph's arrival in prison with these words:

> He sent a man before them—
> Joseph—who was sold as a slave.
> They hurt his feet with fetters,
> He was laid in irons.
> Until the time that his word came to pass,
> The word of the LORD tested him (Psalm 105:17–19).

But Joseph's real character shines out, even in the darkness of the dungeon. He held fast his faith and patience; his years of faithful service had been most cruelly repaid, yet this did not render him morose or distrustful. He had the peace that comes from conscious innocence, and he trusted his case with God. He did not brood upon his own wrongs, but forgot his sorrow in trying to lighten the sorrows of others. He found a work to do, even in the prison. God was preparing him in the school of affliction for greater usefulness, and he did not refuse the needful discipline. In the prison, witnessing the results of oppression and tyranny and the effects of crime, he learned lessons of justice, sympathy, and mercy, that prepared him to exercise power with wisdom and compassion.[4]

Returning to the biblical account: "But the LORD was with Joseph and showed him mercy, and He gave him favor in the sight of the keeper of the prison. And the keeper of the prison committed to Joseph's hand all the prisoners who were in the prison; whatever they did there, it was his doing. The keeper of the prison did not look into anything that was under Joseph's authority, because the LORD was with him; and whatever he did, the LORD made it prosper" (Genesis 39:21–23).

Once again, good conduct and a willing spirit paved the way for Joseph: his diligence, his benevolence, and his respect for others gained him the sympathy of the one in charge of the prison. The jailer, recognizing the talents and responsibility of this youth, placed him as an administrator of the prison, even though Joseph was a prisoner. This seems incredible! Once again, the slave gains a position of influence in the environment he's in. In the midst of his misfortune, another victory is scored. So it was and so it shall be; this story will be repeated in all those who determine to be like Joseph.

The Bible then relates an incident that, with the passing of time, resulted in a blessing for Joseph. Two servants of the king of Egypt, the cupbearer (or butler) and the baker of the palace, were put in prison with Joseph:

It came to pass after these things that the butler and the baker of the king of Egypt offended their lord, the king of Egypt. And Pharaoh was angry with his two officers, the chief butler and the chief baker. So he put them in custody in the house of the captain of the guard, in the prison, the place where Joseph was confined. And the captain of the guard charged Joseph with them, and he served them; so they were in custody for a while.

Then the butler and the baker of the king of Egypt, who were confined in the prison, had a dream, both of them, each man's dream in one night and each man's dream with its own interpretation. And Joseph came in to them in the morning and looked at them, and saw that they were sad. So he asked Pharaoh's officers who were with him in the custody of his lord's house, saying, "Why do you look so sad today?"

And they said to him, "We each have had a dream, and there is no interpreter of it."

So Joseph said to them, "Do not interpretations belong to God? Tell them to me, please."

Then the chief butler told his dream to Joseph, and said to him, "Behold, in my dream a vine was before me, and in the vine were three branches; it was as though it budded, its blossoms shot forth, and its clusters brought forth ripe grapes. Then Pharaoh's cup was in my hand; and I took the grapes and pressed them into Pharaoh's cup, and placed the cup in Pharaoh's hand."

And Joseph said to him, "This is the interpretation of it: The three branches are three days. Now within three days Pharaoh will lift up your head and restore you to your place, and you will put Pharaoh's cup in his hand according to the former manner, when you were his butler. But remember me when it is well with you, and please show kindness to me; make mention of me to Pharaoh, and get me out of this house. For indeed I was stolen away from the land of the Hebrews; and also I have done nothing here that they should put me into the dungeon."

When the chief baker saw that the interpretation was good, he said to Joseph, "I also was in my dream, and there were three white baskets on my head. In the uppermost basket were all kinds of baked goods for Pharaoh, and the birds ate them out of the basket on my head."

So Joseph answered and said, "This is the interpretation of it: The three baskets are three days. Within three days Pharaoh will lift off your head from you and hang you on a tree; and the birds will eat your flesh from you."

Now it came to pass on the third day, which was Pharaoh's birthday, that he made a feast for all his servants; and he lifted up the head of the chief butler and of the chief baker among his servants. Then he restored the chief butler to his butlership again, and he placed the cup in Pharaoh's hand. But he hanged the chief baker, as Joseph had interpreted to them. Yet the chief butler did not remember Joseph, but forgot him (Genesis 40:1–23).

Even though the king's cupbearer had initially expressed much gratitude to Joseph for explaining the meaning of his dream, and he saw his dream fulfilled precisely according to Joseph's interpretation, he still failed to remember his benefactor once he was freed from prison. And Joseph had to remain in prison for another two years. He lost the hope that had sprung up in his heart; in the midst of so many trials and vicissitudes, another thorn was added—sadness in the face of ingratitude.[5]

Why is it so hard for human beings to be grateful? Why do we so quickly forget the acts of kindness and gifts received? Let's not allow this to happen in our lives. Let's reserve a place in our hearts to remember and recognize people who have shown us kindness at some point in our lives. I have what I call my "gratitude list." It is fairly long, because there are a good number of people who have done kind deeds for my family and me. And those who do good toward me and mine, especially my children, will have my gratitude forever. I firmly believe that the debt of gratitude is one that can never be fully repaid. Let us not be slow to recognize that certain people have shown us acts of love and have done truly significant favors for us. Others may have simply shown acts of kindness, but the total sum of all the goodness is yet to be revealed. The proportion of good deeds received will surely outweigh the bad deeds committed against us.

This psychological and spiritual exercise will restore to us much of our lost trust in humanity. We will realize that not everyone is full of malice and pettiness. Not everyone goes around looking to pick a fight or to hurt others simply for their enjoyment. I thank God for all the good people who know what love, sympathy, and empathy are. I know that we will come across people who do not know how to, or who cannot, behave themselves in a kind and respectful way; but when that happens, try to remain composed and remember the words of the following poem by Amado Nervo:

If a Thorn Pricks Me
I draw back from the needle
But I do not hate it.
When envious pettiness
Nails in me its darts of rancor,
Quietly I withdraw my foot, and make my departure
For a gentler place
Of love and goodness.
Grudges? What good are they?
What does rancor achieve?
Neither wounds restored
Nor wrongs corrected.
My rose garden barely has time to produce flowers
And lavishes no sap
In sharp little jabs.
If my enemy passes near my rosebushes,
He will take the roses
Of the softest essence;
And you will notice in them
A vivacious red,

It will be from that blood
That yesterday's malevolence
Drew forth so cruelly
And today the rosebush returns
Transformed into a blossoming peace.[6]

Let me share with you as an example, just a part of my own gratitude list:

My List of Gratitude

Name   **Reason for being grateful**

1. Johnny and Clara Ramírez _____

2. Pedro and Isolina Novales_____

3. Eugenio and Mayda Jorge_____

4. Fernando Paulín _____

5. Julian Rumayor _____

6. Juan Puyol _____

7. Pedro and Amarilis Hernández_____

8. Robert W. Boggess _____

I invite you to make and keep a gratitude list. This is one of the best medi-cines for the soul. When you feel sad or offended, when you think that you are alone, or when discouragement calls at your door, take a fresh look at your list, and there you will find reasons to smile again. You will feel motivated to do kind things to those around you, and because of that, the world will be a little better.

---

1. White, *Patriarchs and Prophets*, 214, 217.
2. Ibid., 217.
3. See ibid., 218.
4. Ibid.
5. See ibid., 219.
6. Translation of Amada Nervo, "Si una espina me hiere."

Chapter 7

From Prison to
the Government Palace

And Pharaoh said to his servants,
"Can we find such a one as this,
a man in whom is the Spirit of God?"
—Genesis 41:38

Teacher," Godofredo [Godfrey] asked in his best vernacular, "how many years did Joseph 'haul' in the 5 of Egypt?" (In Cuba, our prison was known as the 5.)

Everyone laughed at the way he framed the question. Godofredo was, in my estimation, the most "innocent" one of our entire group, and he was always counting the days until he would get out of prison. He tearfully longed for his little farm in the mountains of Candelaria. All he wanted was to be with his wife and his boys, to go to sleep when the chickens did and to rise at the crowing of the rooster. He was an uneducated farmer, already past middle age, but strong as a bull and just as brave. He was serving a sentence of twenty-five years. He was put in prison after he was caught slaughtering one of his cattle just to feed his family. He often snorted angrily: "The animal was mine. I didn't steal it from anybody! I was not selling the meat. I was salting it to preserve it for the entire year, just as my father and grandfather always did before me. It was so my wife, my children, and my grandchildren would have food to eat."

Under the laws of the socialist government, killing cattle was, and still is, prohibited, even if the cattle are your property. The sentence was five years imprisonment; but Godofredo—"Dressed Beef" as they called him in prison—in the first month after arriving had the misfortune of getting into an argument with a guard. When the guard hit him with the butt of a rifle, Godofredo yanked his rifle away, knocked him to the ground, and bashed his head against the floor; the guard did not survive. Godofredo was tried again, and his sentence was increased to a total of twenty-five years. He was sent to the Lion's den because he was considered dangerous, and in truth, he could be if he was provoked. But what caused him to despair the most was thinking that when the time of his release came, if he remained alive that long, he would have to use a cane to walk out and he would never again be able to cultivate his land, milk his cows, or ride his horse. I said in my heart, *Here is another injustice.* If Godofredo had remained in his home, feeding his family, cultivating his land, milking his cows, and riding his horse, he probably would have never become a murderer, but only God knows.

Trying to bring some hope to his angry and anguished spirit, I said, "Brother Godofredo, even though Joseph struggled to maintain his hope, he clung to his faith, and although it was very difficult to get out of that prison, almost as difficult as getting out of here, with God nothing is impossible! That's what happened to Joseph, and now let's continue the story if we may:

"But a divine hand was about to open the prison gates. The king of Egypt had in one night two dreams, apparently pointing to the same event and seeming to foreshadow some great calamity. He could not determine their significance, yet they continued to trouble his mind. The magicians and wise men of his realm could give no interpretation. The king's perplexity and distress increased, and terror spread throughout his palace. The general agitation recalled to the chief butler's mind the circumstances of his own dream; with it came the memory of Joseph, and a pang of remorse for his forgetfulness and ingratitude. He at once informed the king how his own dream and that of the chief baker had been interpreted by a Hebrew captive, and how the predictions had been fulfilled.

"It was humiliating to Pharaoh to turn away from the magicians and wise men of his kingdom to consult an alien and a slave, but he was ready to accept the lowliest service if his troubled mind might find relief. Joseph was immediately sent for; he put off his prison attire, and shaved himself, for his hair had grown long during the period of his disgrace and confinement. He was then conducted to the presence of the king.[1]

"And Pharaoh said to Joseph, 'I have had a dream, and there is no one who can interpret it. But I have heard it said of you that you can understand a dream, to interpret it.'

"So Joseph answered Pharaoh, saying, 'It is not in me; God will give Pharaoh an answer of peace' (Genesis 41:15, 16).

"Here Joseph was emphatic; this was not a guessing game. No man can interpret the dreams of another, for no man knows the future, and we should not be fooled by people who claim to know what belongs only to God.

"Many people make their decisions based on horoscopes or the views of soothsayers and fortune-tellers. Beware! God has given us intelligence, the power of reasoning, and the wise counsels in the Bible to help us in the process of making our daily decisions. The gift of prophecy exists, but it is a gift from God. Remember that not all dreams are prophetic. Some dreams are the result of eating food at the wrong hours of the night, so we should not pretend to be prophets when we suffer indigestion. It would be foolish to invent fanciful interpretations for every common dream that our natural thought processes produce; that is not the divine plan. Pharaoh's wise men, astrologers, and fortune-tellers could not decipher his dreams; they were ineffective in this situation simply because God was the One who had given the ruler of the most powerful nation in that region a message designed for preserving lives. The revelation of future events belongs only to God, and when He wants to communicate a message to someone, He makes it understood with impactful and convincing clarity through His prophets.

"Joseph was a prophet of God, and he was willing to listen to the king's dream, confident that God would give him the interpretation.

"Then Pharaoh said to Joseph: 'Behold, in my dream I stood on the bank of the river. Suddenly seven cows came up out of the river, fine looking and fat; and they fed in the meadow. Then behold, seven other cows came up after them, poor and very ugly and gaunt, such ugliness as I have never seen in all the land of Egypt. And the gaunt and ugly cows ate up the first seven, the fat cows. When they had eaten them up, no one would have known that they had eaten them, for they were just as ugly as at the beginning. So I awoke. Also I saw in my dream, and suddenly seven heads came up on one stalk, full and good. Then behold, seven heads, withered, thin, and blighted by the east wind, sprang up after them. And the thin heads devoured the seven good heads. So I told this to the magicians, but there was no one who could explain it to me.'

"Then Joseph said to Pharaoh, 'The dreams of Pharaoh are one; God has shown Pharaoh what He is about to do: The seven good cows are seven years, and the seven good heads are seven years; the dreams are one. And the seven thin and ugly cows which came up after them are seven years, and the seven empty heads blighted by the east wind are seven years of famine. This is the thing which I have spoken to Pharaoh. God has shown Pharaoh what He is about to do. Indeed seven years of great plenty will come throughout all the land of Egypt; but after them seven years of famine will arise, and all the plenty will be forgotten in the land of Egypt; and the famine will deplete the land. So the plenty will not be known in the land because of the famine following, for it will be very severe. And the dream was repeated to Pharaoh twice because the thing is established by God, and God will shortly bring it to pass.

" 'Now therefore, let Pharaoh select a discerning and wise man, and set him over the land of Egypt. Let Pharaoh do this, and let him appoint officers over the land, to collect one-fifth of the produce of the land of Egypt in the seven plentiful years. And let them gather all the food of those good years that are coming, and store up grain under the authority of Pharaoh, and let them keep food in the cities. Then that food shall be as a reserve for the land for the seven years of famine which shall be in the land of Egypt, that the land may not perish during the famine.'

"So the advice was good in the eyes of Pharaoh and in the eyes of all his servants (verses 17–37).

"Who could be trusted with such a great responsibility? The preservation of the nation depended on the wisdom of this choice. After much consideration and after listening to the recommendation of the cupbearer, the king decided to offer Joseph the important position. Pharaoh made Joseph the administrator of the entire nation, second only to himself. He even took off his signet ring and put it on Joseph's hand; he dressed him in fine linen garments and ordered Joseph's new position to be declared publicly.

"He made him lord of his house,
And ruler of all his possessions,
To bind his princes at his pleasure,
And teach his elders wisdom (Psalm 105:21, 22).

"I would like to have seen the reactions of Potiphar and his crafty wife when they heard the news. Perhaps they panicked, wondering what might befall them now that Joseph was in a position of great power; but nowhere in the Bible does it say that Joseph took revenge on them. A person with noble principles such as Joseph possessed, a person who is good and God-fearing, does not use revenge as a weapon. A good person knows how to forgive and leaves vengeance in the hands of God; it is He who knows the hearts and motives of humans.

"Joseph endured very well the trials of his life, both in prosperity and in adversity. 'The same fidelity to God was manifest when he stood in the palace of the Pharaohs as when in a prisoner's cell. He was still a stranger in a heathen land, separated from his kindred, the worshipers of God; but he fully believed that the divine hand had directed his steps, and in constant reliance upon God he faithfully discharged the duties of his position. Through Joseph the attention of the king and great men of Egypt was directed to the true God.'[2]

"You may ask how it was possible that this man, who was sold by his brothers; a slave to Potiphar; falsely accused by the wicked wife of his master; unjustly jailed; forgotten by the king's cupbearer, whom he had helped and encouraged;

after so many trials and mistreatments and so much anguish, could still demonstrate such an admirable strength of character that continued to carry him through all these misfortunes.

" 'How was Joseph enabled to make such a record of firmness of character, uprightness, and wisdom? . . . He had consulted duty rather than inclination;'[3] and maintained his integrity. His simple trust and noble disposition bore splendid fruit in all his actions. When people decide to live in communion with God and according to His will and allow that determination to govern all areas of their lives, their minds become disciplined to choose goodness and duty before evil and pleasure. 'The formation of a noble character is the work of a lifetime and must be the result of diligent and persevering effort. God gives opportunities; success depends on the use made of them.'[4]

"Yes, my friends, no matter the circumstances life presents us with, or the ones we have gotten ourselves into, there is always an opportunity for us to live responsibly and to rectify our mistakes and come into harmony with God and that which is right."

"I would like to be like Joseph!" Brother Gravarán said enthusiastically.

"That's not easy," Brother Almansa grumbled, "and much less in this Lion's den."

Godofredo, always thinking of his family and his farm up in the mountains, wistfully asked, "What happened to Joseph's aging father and his brothers? Did they ever see each other again?"

Joseph's brothers

" 'At the very opening of the fruitful years began preparations for the approaching famine. Under the direction of Joseph, immense storehouses were erected in all the principal places throughout the land of Egypt, and ample arrangements were made for preserving the surplus of the expected harvest.'[5] In this way, during the seven years of plenty, the Egyptians continued to store up grain, until the amount of grain stored was incalculable.

"And then the seven years of famine began, according to Joseph's prediction. Although in all the regions surrounding Egypt, there was widespread hunger, in the land of Egypt, there was more than enough food. 'So when all the land of Egypt was famished, the people cried to Pharaoh for bread. Then Pharaoh said to all the Egyptians, "Go to Joseph; whatever he says to you, do" ' (Genesis 41:55).

"But the very severe hunger also spread throughout the land of Canaan, where Joseph's father lived with his brothers and their families. When they heard of the abundance of provisions in Egypt, ten of Jacob's sons traveled there to buy grain to feed their families. Upon arrival, they presented themselves before the governor of the land and bowed before him.[6]

"Joseph recognized his brothers, but they didn't realize that the governor with the Egyptian name was a being who was very familiar to them. When Jacob's sons bowed to greet the high-ranking Egyptian governor, Joseph remembered his dreams, and many past scenes with his family came vividly before him. He longed to see his father and worried that he didn't see among his brothers the youngest of Jacob's sons, Benjamin. He feared for his younger brother's whereabouts; he feared that Benjamin had been a victim of the cruelty of those men. So he decided to find out the truth. 'You are spies! You have come to see the nakedness of the land!' (Genesis 42:9). Twice he accused them of spying, in order to verify that they were telling him the truth, since he knew how unreliable his brothers were. They responded that they were not spies, but 'the sons of one man in the land of Canaan; and in fact, the youngest is with our father today, and one is no more' (verse 13).

"Joseph pretended to doubt the veracity of what they said and put them to the test: 'You shall not leave this place unless your youngest brother comes here' (verse 15). If they did not agree to this, then they would be treated as spies. Giving them time to think, 'he put them all together in prison three days' (verse 17). But this increased the anxiety of Jacob's sons: the time they needed to bring Benjamin to Egypt prolonged the waiting of their families, who were suffering hunger from the lack of food. Moreover, which of them would undertake the journey alone, leaving his brothers in prison? What would he say to his father? Besides, the brothers could be condemned to death or made slaves. And if they brought Benjamin to Egypt, it might be only to suffer the same fate as his brothers. They decided to stay there and suffer together, rather than increase their father's sadness with the loss of his only remaining son by Rachel. So they remained in prison three days.

"During the years since Joseph had been separated from his brothers, these sons of Jacob had changed in character. Envious, turbulent, deceptive, cruel, and revengeful they had been; but now, when tested by adversity, they were shown to be unselfish, true to one another, devoted to their father, and, themselves middle-aged men, subject to his authority.

"The three days in the Egyptian prison were days of bitter sorrow as the brothers reflected upon their past sins. Unless Benjamin could be produced their conviction as spies appeared certain, and they had little hope of getting their father's consent to Benjamin's absence. On the third day Joseph caused the brothers to be brought before him. He dared not detain them longer. Already his father and the families with him might be suffering for food.[7]

" 'Do this and live, for I fear God: If you are honest men, let one of your brothers be confined to your prison house; but you, go and carry grain for the famine of your houses. And bring your youngest brother to me; so your words will be verified, and you shall not die' (verses 18–20). They agreed to accept this proposal, while expressing little hope that their father would let Benjamin return with them to Egypt.

"So then Joseph's brothers began to reproach one another with loud voices, thinking that the Egyptian governor could not understand what they were saying. And after mutual accusations and expressions of remorse, they said, 'We are truly guilty concerning our brother, for we saw the anguish of his soul when he pleaded with us, and we would not hear; therefore this distress has come upon us' (verse 21). Reuben, who had wanted to set him free in Dothan, added, 'Did I not speak to you, saying, "Do not sin against the boy"; and you would not listen? Therefore behold, his blood is now required of us' (verse 22). Joseph, who had been listening, could not control his emotions, and he went out and wept. 'On his return he commanded that Simeon be bound before them and again committed to prison. In the cruel treatment of their brother, Simeon had been the instigator and chief actor, and it was for this reason that the choice fell upon him.'[8]

"When Joseph allowed his brothers to return home, he ordered that their money for payment of the food be hidden in their grain sacks. He also ordered that they be given sufficient fodder for their animals for the journey. Later, along the way, when the brothers found the money in their sacks, instead of considering it a blessing from the Lord, they worried, thinking that God was punishing them all the more because of their sins.

"That is the mental condition of those who do not have the peace of God in their conscience: everything that happens becomes a source of anxiety and concern.

"Jacob welcomed his nine sons home, but he was full of alarm and suspicion. The intentions of the governor of Egypt did not seem at all good, and the old man refused for a long time to allow his youngest son, Benjamin, to make the trip to Egypt. Nevertheless, as time passed, the famine grew worse, and it seriously threatened the survival of the family.

"So Jacob could not withhold consent any longer, and he ordered his sons to prepare for the trip. He also commanded them to take the governor a gift of the things that the country could still provide, even though devastated as it was by hunger: a small portion of balm, a bit of honey, spices and myrrh, nuts and almonds, and double the amount of money. When his sons were ready to make the uncertain journey, the elderly father stood up and, raising his arms to heaven, uttered this prayer: 'May God Almighty give you mercy before the man, that he may release your other brother and Benjamin. If I am bereaved, I am bereaved!' (Genesis 43:14).

"When the governor saw them again, the brothers presented him with their gifts and humbly bowed before him, and Joseph again remembered his dreams. After Joseph greeted his visitors, he was quick to ask about their father: 'Is your father well . . . ? Is he still alive?' (verse 27). His eyes fell on Benjamin, and he said, 'God be gracious to you, my son' (verse 29). But overwhelmed by his feelings of tenderness, 'his heart yearned for his brother; so Joseph made haste and sought somewhere to weep. And he went into his chamber and wept there' (verse 30).

"After regaining his self-control, Joseph came back and gathered together with his brothers and ordered that the table be prepared, so they could eat together. He and the Egyptians ate separately from his brothers 'because the Egyptians could not eat food with the Hebrews, for that is an abomination to the Egyptians' (verse 32). But when they were seated at the table, the brothers were surprised to see that they were seated in the exact order according to their ages. So Joseph 'took servings to them from before him, but Benjamin's serving was five times as much as any of theirs' (verse 34). Through this demonstration of favor to Benjamin, Joseph wanted to see if the older brothers felt the same envy and hatred for the youngest that they had expressed toward him. Still believing that Joseph did not understand their language, the brothers freely conversed with one another. In this manner, they revealed their true sentiments toward their brother, the governor of Egypt.

"But Joseph wanted to test his brothers further, and he ordered that his own silver cup be secretly placed in the sack of the youngest brother upon their departure.

" 'Joyfully they set out on their return. Simeon and Benjamin were with them, their animals were laden with grain, and all felt that they had safely escaped the perils that had seemed to surround them. But they had only reached the outskirts of the city when they were overtaken by the governor's steward,'[9] who directed a shocking accusation at them: 'Why have you repaid evil for good? Is not this the one [the cup] from which my lord drinks, and with which he indeed practices divination? You have done evil in so doing' (Genesis 44:4, 5).

"It was assumed that the cup had the capacity of detecting poisonous substances poured into it. In those times, vessels of this kind were highly valued as a protection against poisoning.[10]

"To the steward's accusation, the travelers replied,

" 'Why does my lord say these words? . . . With whomever of your servants it is found, let him die, and we also will be my lord's slaves.'

"And he [Joseph's steward] said, 'Now also let it be according to your words' (verses 7–10).

"But the cup was found in Benjamin's sack. The brothers tore their clothes as a sign of grief and slowly returned to the city. According to his own oath, Benjamin was condemned.

"Let's allow the dramatic biblical narrative to tell us how that dialogue between the governor of Egypt and his brothers went:

"And Joseph said to them, 'What deed is this you have done? Did you not know that such a man as I can certainly practice divination?'

"Then Judah said, 'What shall we say to my lord? What shall we speak? Or how shall we clear ourselves? God has found out the iniquity of your servants; here we are, my lord's slaves, both we and he also with whom the cup was found.'

"But he said, 'Far be it from me that I should do so; the man in whose hand the cup was found, he shall be my slave. And as for you, go up in peace to your father.'

"Then Judah came near to him and said: 'O my lord, please let your servant speak a word in my lord's hearing, and do not let your anger burn against your servant; for you are even like Pharaoh. My lord asked his servants, saying, "Have you a father or a brother?" And we said to my lord, "We have a father, an old man, and a child of his old age, who is young; his brother is dead, and he alone is left of his mother's children, and his father loves him." Then you said to your servants, "Bring him down to me, that I may set my eyes on him." And we said to my lord, "The lad cannot leave his father, for if he should leave his father, his father would die." But you said to your servants, "Unless your youngest brother comes down with you, you shall see my face no more."

" 'So it was, when we went up to your servant my father, that we told him the words of my lord. And our father said, "Go back and buy us a little food." But we said, "We cannot go down; if our youngest brother is with us, then we will go down; for we may not see the man's face unless our youngest brother is with us." Then your servant my father said to us, "You know that my wife bore me two sons; and the one went out from me, and I said, 'Surely he is torn to pieces'; and I have not seen him since. But if you take this one also from me, and calamity befalls him, you shall bring down my gray hair with sorrow to the grave."

" 'Now therefore, when I come to your servant my father, and the lad is not with us, since his life is bound up in the lad's life, it will happen, when he sees that the lad is not with us, that he will die. So your servants will bring down the gray hair of your servant our father with sorrow to the grave. For your servant became surety for the lad to my father, saying, "If I do not bring him back to you, then I shall bear the blame before my father forever." Now therefore, please let your servant remain instead of the lad as a slave to my lord, and let the lad go up with his brothers. For how shall I go up to my father if the lad is not with me, lest perhaps I see the evil that would come upon my father?' (verses 15–34).

" 'Joseph was satisfied. He had seen in his brothers the fruits of true repentance. Upon hearing Judah's noble offer he gave orders that all but these men should withdraw; then, weeping aloud,'[11] he exclaimed, ' "I am Joseph; does my father still live?" (Genesis 45:3).

" 'His brothers stood motionless, dumb with fear and amazement. The ruler of Egypt their brother Joseph, whom they had envied and would have murdered, and finally sold as a slave! All their ill treatment of him passed before them. They remembered how they had despised his dreams and had labored to prevent their fulfillment.'[12] Now, however, they had participated in fulfilling those very dreams, and here they were, face-to-face with Joseph, the governor of Egypt.

"Joseph then asked them to come near and said to them, 'I am Joseph your brother, whom you sold into Egypt. But now, do not therefore be grieved or angry with yourselves because you sold me here; for God sent me before you to preserve life' (verses 4, 5). And with Pharaoh's consent, they were provided with carriages to bring Jacob and all of Joseph's brothers' families to Egypt, to live in the fertile grazing land of Goshen."

At this point in the story, practically all of my cellmates were in tears, and I had the opportunity to invite them to be like Joseph. I pointed out that Joseph was an example of Jesus in his integrity and his tremendous forgiving heart.

And so, as a new day was beginning to dawn, I ended the longest sermon of my life. None of my cellmates fell asleep!

I closed with a Bible text that is a proverb that we should all cherish in our minds and hearts: "Behold, the fear of the Lord, that is wisdom, and to depart from evil is understanding" (Job 28:28).

---

1. White, *Patriarchs and Prophets*, 219, 220.

2. Ibid., 222.

3. Ibid.

4. Ibid., 223.

5. Ibid., 224.

6. See ibid.

7. Ibid., 225.

8. Ibid., 226.

9. Ibid., 229.

10. See ibid.

11. Ibid., 230.

12. Ibid.

Chapter 8

The Man Who Killed Dracula

"I say to you that likewise there will be more joy in heaven over one sinner who repents than over ninety-nine just persons who need no repentance."
—Luke 15:7

The next day Heaven seemed to smile upon us insofar as our better living conditions, at least momentarily. By an order of the sergeant in charge of operations, we were moved to a "normal" cell, although still within the same Lion's den. It was kind of a galley, where each of us would have our own bunks for sleeping, and we would enjoy individual bedsheets if we took good care of them. We would have access to communal bathrooms with very rustic toilets with some privacy at least, but to me, they seemed as nice as those of a luxury hotel compared to our previous situation. We were denied access to the common mess hall because it was considered a high-risk place, but at least we received our plates in our hands, and the meager ration was relatively clean. I thanked the Lord!

Disturbing rumors

Disturbing rumors began to reach my ears the second day in the new residence. There in the Lion's den, in addition to the guards and other dangers, resided a certain individual whose name was only mentioned in whispers, yet was well known to everyone in the prison community. He was feared and respected, though not everyone had seen him face-to-face. I, of course, did not know him, though it was not the first time I had heard of him. He was called "the Lion," and within that section of the prison, his word was law. Oddly enough, even the hall guards tried to please him. He had a cell all to himself, and everyone said he was the boss of section 4. Some spoke of him with fear: "That man was the one who killed Dracula."

Nicolas, "the Russian," and Godofredo, "Dressed Beef," came up to me with an air of concern: "Teacher, we cannot let you out of our sight even for a moment. It looks like we're in for some trouble! Do you think that God will help us fight in self-defense?"

"But why? What's wrong?" I asked.

"That man," Nicolas said half scared, "the one who they say killed Dracula, says he wants to see you face-to-face, and we're afraid for you. One of his rules is that there cannot be two bosses here. And if someone is head of a certain group, then that is one too many, so one will have to be taken out and the same for anyone who defends him. The inmates say that the guards let the Lion punish the prisoners who give them problems or ones they especially dislike.

"And they also say," he continued with a deep sigh, looking me straight in the eyes, "that nobody has ever been able to win a fight with him ever since the night he killed Dracula. Besides, after he killed Dracula, they gave him his cell, because Dracula was the boss before the Lion came. Some prisoners remember that twelve years ago this section was called 'Dracula's lair.' "

I have to confess that even though I told the men not to worry because God was with us, inside my scrawny 120 pounds of humanity was not prepared to come face-to-face with a lion—the winner of many fights, a frightening criminal, an instrument of corrupt guards, a man who had killed Dracula himself! Besides, fighting was never my sport or vocation.

I believe that my body is the temple of the Holy Spirit, and nobody has the right to abuse it. But neither could I run, and there was nowhere to hide. So as I always do, I turned to God and said, "I don't know what life has in store for me, but I place myself in Your hands. And if You want to save me from the Lion's clutches, please do so! Lord, if something should happen to me, please watch over my dear Celita and our unborn baby. But please, Lord, don't let the good work begun in this place for the prisoners be destroyed by the hands of the adversary!"

Most of the rest of that day I kept returning to that prayer, and I kept searching in my mind for Bible passages that would help me in the hour of trial that was looming. That afternoon, like every other afternoon, I was to speak to the group as was now our custom. Everyone was tense and worried but had to be prepared for what was to happen. And then, what God put in my heart was the story of Daniel and his encounter with the lions, just as it is told in chapter 6 of his book. I told the prisoners the story more or less as follows:

"Starting with the reign of Nebuchadnezzar, king of Babylon, one of the four great empires of the ancient world, the nation of Israel suffered about seventy years of captivity. Among the Jewish captives, there were a few youth true to godly principles who were taken to Babylon to serve the king in various tasks. Among this group, there were young 'men who were as true as steel to principle, who would not be corrupted by selfishness, but who would honor the God'[1] in the midst of idolatry, wealth, and the prevailing corruption of the pagan environment of the most powerful nation of that time. They decided to honor God whatever the personal cost, even at the risk of their very lives. 'Never were they to compromise with idolaters; their faith and their name as worshipers of the living God they were to bear as a high honor. And this they did. In prosperity and in adversity they honored God, and God honored them.' "[2]

"Yes, actually, the Jews condemn all forms of idolatry," Brother Almansa broke in.

"But the message I want to leave you with goes beyond the simple prohibition of worshiping idols. I am talking about how to face fear," I responded and then continued. " 'Among those who maintained their allegiance to God were Daniel and his three companions—illustrious examples of what men may become who unite with the God of wisdom and power. From the comparative simplicity of their Jewish home, these youth of royal line were taken to the most magnificent of cities and into the court of the world's greatest monarch.'[3] Daniel served under the kings of Babylon as a wise counselor, political administrator, and spiritual guide with so much integrity and accountability that when the first empire was overthrown by the Medo-Persians, he was once again elevated to honored positions in the second empire. The Bible says that 'it pleased Darius to set over the kingdom one hundred and twenty satraps, to be over the whole kingdom; and over these, three governors, of whom Daniel was one, that the satraps might give account to them, so that the king would suffer no loss. Then this Daniel distinguished himself above the governors and satraps, because an excellent spirit was in him; and the king gave thought to setting him over the whole realm' [Daniel 6:1–3]. 'The honors bestowed upon Daniel excited the jealousy of the leading men of the kingdom, and they sought for occasion of complaint against him.'[4] But they could find no reason for it, 'because he was faithful; nor was there any error or fault found in him' " (verse 4).

"Well, here it's the contrary. The more corrupt a person is, the higher his position," Godofredo grumbled. The rest of the inmates laughed at the humor and astuteness of Godofredo's words.

After a brief silence, I continued. " 'Daniel's blameless conduct excited still further the jealousy of his enemies.'[5] They were forced to admit: 'We shall not find any charge against this Daniel unless we find it against him concerning the law of his God' [verse 5]. Therefore, the presidents and princes, scheming together, devised a plan by which they hoped to accomplish the prophet's destruction. They resolved to ask the king to sign a decree that they cunningly prepared, prohibiting anyone in the kingdom from asking anything of God or man except of King Darius, for thirty days. The violation of this decree would result in throwing the guilty culprit into a den of lions."

"The lion's den!" shouted someone I couldn't identify. Everyone laughed.

"Yes, indeed, the lion's den," I responded. " 'Accordingly, the princes prepared such a decree, and presented it to Darius for his signature.' Appealing to his vanity, he was convinced that the implementation of this edict would greatly increase his honor and authority. Not knowing the subtle purpose of the princes, 'the king did not discern their animosity as revealed in the decree, and yielding to their flattery, he signed it.'[6]

"Daniel's enemies left the presence of Darius rejoicing in the trap that was now well prepared for the servant of the Lord. But even though Daniel readily recognized the evil purpose of the decree, he did not change his conduct in any one single detail. Why would he cease praying now, when he needed prayer more than ever? He was prepared to give up his life rather than waver in his trust in God's help. Calmly he went about fulfilling his duties as president of the princes; and when it was time for him to pray, he went into his bedroom and with the windows open toward Jerusalem, as was his custom, offered his petition to the God of heaven. He did not seek to conceal this act. Although he knew very well the consequences of his faithfulness to God, his spirit did not hesitate. He refused to give in to those who were plotting his ruin. Not even in the slightest appearance would he sever his relationship with Heaven. In all cases in which the king exercised rightful authority, Daniel would obey him; but neither the king nor his decree could divert his loyalty to the King of kings."[7]

"That is a brave man," Nicolas said.

"Yes, of course, in this way, the prophet declared with serene and humble boldness that no earthly power has the right to stand between one's soul and God," I responded.

Those of us who were gathered there knew very well the meaning of these last words. Not just any power, but neither any government nor state, has the right to dictate a religious conscience. The free exercise of a personal relationship with God is an absolute right.

I continued the story.

"Surrounded by idolaters, he [Daniel] was a faithful witness to this truth. His dauntless adherence to right was a bright light in the moral darkness of that heathen court. Daniel stands before the world today a worthy example of Christian fearlessness and fidelity.

"For an entire day the princes watched Daniel. Three times they saw him go to his chamber, and three times they heard his voice lifted in earnest intercession to God. The next morning they laid their complaint before the king. Daniel, his most honored and faithful statesman, had set the royal decree at defiance.[8]

"They reminded the king: ' "Have you not signed a decree that every man who petitions any god or man within thirty days, except you, O king, shall be cast into the den of lions?" The king answered and said, "The thing is true, according to the law of the Medes and Persians, which does not alter" ' [verse 12]. Then triumphantly they informed Darius of the conduct of his most trusted adviser.

They exclaimed, 'That Daniel, who is one of the captives from Judah, does not show due regard for you, O king, or for the decree that you have signed, but makes his petition three times a day' [verse 13].

"When he heard these words, the king immediately saw the trap that they had laid for his faithful servant. 'He saw that it was not zeal for kingly glory and honor, but jealousy against Daniel, that had lead to the proposal for a royal decree.'9 The biblical narrative says that 'the king, when he heard these words, was greatly displeased with himself' for the part he had played in this wrong-doing, and 'he labored till the going down of the sun to deliver him' [verse 14]. Anticipating this effort by the king, the princes said to him, 'Know, O king, that it is the law of the Medes and Persians that no decree or statute which the king establishes may be changed' [verse 15]. Although hastily enacted, the decree was unalterable and must be fulfilled.10

"Then the king commanded, and they brought Daniel and cast him into the lions' den. The king said to Daniel, 'Your God, whom you serve continually, He will deliver you' [verse 16]. A stone was put in front of the den, and the king himself sealed it with his ring and the rings of his princes so that nothing concerning Daniel would be changed. Then 'the king went to his palace and spent the night fasting; and no musicians were brought before him. Also his sleep went from him' during those fateful hours [verse 18].

" 'God did not prevent Daniel's enemies from casting him into the lions' den; He permitted evil angels and wicked men to accomplish their purpose; but it was that He might make the deliverance of His servant more marked, and the defeat of the enemies of truth and righteousness more complete.'11 As the psalmist says, 'Surely the wrath of man shall praise You' [Psalm 76:10]. 'Through the courage of this one man who chose to follow right rather than policy, Satan was to be defeated, and the name of God was to be exalted and honored.' "12

"Teacher, what you are saying brings me excitement. Things can be seen in different ways; we sometimes interpret God in the wrong way, but we need to learn to wait and be patient," Nicolas said pensively.

"Yes, indeed, we must allow God to finish painting the whole picture to see the meaning of His strokes. Many times we stop at just a few brushstrokes," I answered, and the men nodded that they had understood my metaphor. "But let's continue with this fascinating story. Early the next morning King Darius quickly made his way to the den of lions, and

"he cried out with a lamenting voice to Daniel. . . . 'Daniel, servant of the living God, has your God, whom you serve continually, been able to deliver you from the lions?'

"Then Daniel said to the king, 'O king, live forever! My God sent His angel and shut the lions' mouths, so that they have not hurt me, because I was found innocent before Him; and also, O king, I have done no wrong before you.'

"Now the king was exceedingly glad for him, and commanded that they should take Daniel up out of the den. So Daniel was taken up out of the den, and no injury whatever was found on him, because he believed in his God [verses 20–23].

"So then the mighty monarch gave orders that all those men who had accused Daniel be cast into the den of lions, and the wild beasts tore them to pieces and devoured them. Then the king sent this edict to all nations and in all the languages spoken in his vast empire:

"I make a decree that in every dominion of my kingdom men must tremble and fear before the God of Daniel.

"For He is the living God,
And steadfast forever;
His kingdom is the one which shall not be destroyed,
And His dominion shall endure to the end.
He delivers and rescues,
And He works signs and wonders
In heaven and on earth,
Who has delivered Daniel from the power of the lions.

"So this Daniel prospered in the reign of Darius and in the reign of Cyrus the Persian " (verses 26–28).

When I had finished the sermon on Daniel, I invited the men to pray, and I told them that God is still God and that He will take care of us if we trust in Him. We were not a gang, and we were not going to have a war with anyone. We were Christians who serve the Living God.

We had barely finished praying when the hall guard came and called my name. He said that another inmate had asked to speak with me in his cell. I asked who it was and why he wanted to talk to me. "It's the Lion," he replied, "and you better go see him. He is sort of like the boss of all the prisoners in this section; and if you offend him, things can get very bad for you."

Fearing for my safety, several of the inmates urged me not to go. "Don't go, Teacher! That man is the devil incarnate! Remember, he is the man who killed Dracula. He has also cracked the skulls of some of the toughest men in this prison."

Maybe it was God giving me courage, or maybe it was that I didn't want a rivalry to form between our new believers and the Lion's people. Like I have said, I'm not a fighter and martyrdom is not among my talents. But I decided to go, and with my heart in my throat, I said to the guard, "Open the door, and take me to him; we will see what we can offer the Lion."

His cell was nearby, just around a corner; it was not as big as our galley, but it was more comfortable and had some furniture that gave it the appearance of a room. There was the dreaded Lion; he was clearly a special inmate, for he lived alone. He was about fifteen years older than I, and he was the only prisoner allowed to keep his hair, which was quite long and blond, resembling a lion's mane. His gaze was fierce but intelligent. He waited for the guard to close the outer doors and then, in a tone that took me by surprise, began to speak words I never expected at all.

"Father! I need to confess! Please, be seated. My name is Leonardo, and I've been in this place for the last twelve years, and I'll most likely be here until the day I die. I've lost all hope."

I wanted to clarify to him that I was not a priest and that all confessions should be directed to God alone and to the people we have wronged. But I decided it would be best to listen to him; interrupting him would have been a mistake and an impossibility. His words were coming out like a torrent, and more than the roar of a lion, they seemed to be a cry of a wounded soul in deep anguish. This fearsome beast was completely broken in spirit. I continued to patiently listen to him.

"A little more than twelve years ago, I ended up here without having committed any crime. I know what you are thinking, that every prisoner says the same thing: 'I didn't do anything'; but in my case, it is true, at least at first. I was young, very idealistic, and, before falling in disgrace, was a successful man at the university. I grew up in a religious home: my parents were practicing Catholics; they never missed Sunday Mass. For the sake of obtaining political benefits following the revolution, I began to abandon my religious beliefs. I joined the Young Communist League. At twenty-four, I was a professor at Central University with a bachelor's degree in physical education, with coaching experience in karate and martial arts. Everybody admired me and loved me, and I had a beautiful, intelligent girlfriend. At that time, Cuba began to receive the cursed help of our Soviet comrades from the Soviet Union, who think they are the owners of our island and the university. As it happened, one of those Soviet professors, a shameless man who spent much of his time making advances and insinuations in the name of free love toward all the girls on campus, crossed my life."

Here he paused his story, as if to take a breath, wanting to forget the origin of his misfortunes, the moment when everything came crashing down. Then he continued.

"One afternoon I was out jogging for my daily exercise and came upon that Russian just as he was violently trying to shove my girlfriend into his car. My girlfriend was fighting back with all her strength. Naturally, I ran over to them, shouting at him to stop. Since he had no words to excuse his actions, he took a swing at me with his clenched fist. In self-defense, I hit back, delivering a solid blow to his shoulder and breaking his collarbone. He fell on the ground shrieking in pain. The police showed up and arrested me for aggression against a Soviet comrade; they accused me of being backward in my thinking. I had no idea that laying a hand on a Russian was such a serious crime. I was given a sentence of five years, and it was recommended that I be placed in a high-security prison to serve as a warning to those who don't value the importance of relations between Cuba and the Soviet Union."

"But how was it that you came here, and why so many years in this section?" I asked him in order to find out the story that was rumored about Dracula. I wanted to know how it had all happened. It wasn't just curiosity. I knew that behind this "wild beast" there was a heart that yearned for justice and love.

"So it was that I was brought here to the 5, because they said this is what I needed in order to 'teach me a lesson.' And I was put in section 4 as my punishment. At that time, the head of this section was a prisoner who held great power and who commanded a dreaded gang inside the prison. He was a degenerate, who was called 'Dracula' by everyone. He was mentally sick. He suffered from syphilis and other venereal diseases, and he had lost all of his upper teeth except for the two long canines that made him look like a vampire; but he was worse than any vampire! As I found out, he paid Hall to bring him the young men who were brought to section 4; there were more than forty men whom he had sodomized, either by seduction or by rape. His sidekicks were always on hand to make sure the victims 'cooperated.' It seemed that these abuses were not known to the prison authorities; if they were known, they never did anything to stop it. I later learned that Dracula had been the instrument used by prison authorities to intimidate and control unruly inmates or those who angered the guards or who failed to adapt to this place.

"That afternoon when I arrived," he continued, staring at me with a tormented look in his eyes, "Hall brazenly shouted out: 'Fresh meat! Fresh meat!' And he added, 'Dracula, I'll sell you this blond pigeon!' All the rest of that afternoon they kept up their bartering racket: 'I'll sell you this pigeon!' Who knows what deal they finally struck, but when night fell, Hall came with orders for me to gather up my things because he had orders to move me to another cell. I was moved into this cursed cell, which was called 'Dracula's lair.' At first, that degenerate man treated me with affection, in order to gain my trust, but soon he began to make more open insinuations and sexual propositions. He told me stories of how well it had gone for other young men who had passed through here. I told him straight out that I was a man and that he had zero possibility with me. Then he tried to force me, so I hit him with a few punches designed to discourage him in his attempt but not to do him any serious harm. Instead, the fool began to scream for Hall: 'Hall, bring me some help! You sold me a pigeon, but it turns out he's a hawk!' And I roared right back, 'I'm not a hawk. I'm a lion! Now leave me alone!' "

"So that's why they call you the Lion," I said, but he ignored me.

"He shamelessly kept screaming for Hall to come open the adjacent cells and let his sidekicks come to help him. When two of his men were let into our cell, they tried reasoning with me: 'Come on, kid, we'll all have a good time. Everyone resists the first time, but soon they like it.' Now I was really getting mad. Those wretches made the mistake of trying to grab me and hold me down. That's when things went bad for them! With my karate and martial arts skills, I was able to fend them off. But they wouldn't give up. That's when my anger turned to fury, and I began to fight to defend my life. But I was afraid of what would happen if I went too far and killed them. I only wanted to knock them out and leave it at that. But, in the heat of the fight, I lost all hesitancy about the consequences; with three demons on my back, I struck to kill. Both gang members ended up dead on the floor. Dracula grabbed a knife and, with crazed eyes, came at me: 'Pigeon (explicative), I'm going to kill you!' I didn't know what to do; I didn't want to kill him, but infuriated as I was, I delivered two punches. Just one such blow would have been enough to finish him off; he fell to the floor like a rag doll. The shouting of his other sidekicks, who wanted to come to his rescue, was deafening. A squad of guards came rushing to the cell to control the situation, but no one dared touch me. That stupid hall guard who had sold me to Dracula didn't have enough intelligence to stay back. As soon as I could reach him, I grabbed him and gave him such a blow to the stomach that he, too, departed this world. He would be selling no more pigeons! They hauled away the four bodies and moved me into solitary confinement.

"I had never killed anyone; all I ever wanted to do was practice karate and martial arts as a sport. It never occurred to me that I would find myself in so desperate a situation as that. I have no idea how long they held me in solitary confinement, but those were weeks of horror. I couldn't sleep at all; every time I started to fall asleep, I would suffer horrific nightmares that scared me out of my wits there on that wet floor. I felt I was going crazy and later I realized that it was true; yes, I was mad. I've been acting like a madman, like a savage."

At that moment, there was a profound silence. Both of us reflected on those events. Once again I thought about how one unfortunate circumstance can twist the destiny of a person. If nothing had happened with that Russian, who would Leonardo be today? After a few minutes that seemed like hours, he continued with his story.

"I think that Satan himself has taken possession of my body and mind all these years! But this is not who I am! I was never like this before. I am living my death, but just can't seem to finish dying.

"Since the guards had lost their punisher, they took me out of solitary confinement one day. They made me bathe and change clothes, and they offered me the very cell where Dracula had lived. My new sentence was thirty years for each of the murders, plus ten years for a revolt within prison walls. Add to that the five years that I was already serving: a total of one hundred and thirty-five years. Add all that to my present age, and you can see that I'll never live long enough to pay all the years of imprisonment to which I have been condemned. I know this perfectly well; for me there is no hope!"

He shook his head like a caged lion, reduced by a trainer to forced obedience. Then Leonardo continued his confession: "I have not been able to speak to a decent person during all these years. Lately I began to feel the need to make confession to a priest. I'm desperate; I don't want to keep living. Here, in this wretched place, I have had to continue to play the role of a murderer, an assassin, the Lion, the man who killed Dracula. But I am sick of it all, and I was thinking about committing suicide. But the afternoon you came to section 4, I recognized that there is something beyond this life. I heard your voice; I saw the light; and I saw all that took place. It left a strange impression on me. Your words still echo here in my mind: *'Lord, Lord God Almighty in battle! Here is Your servant, tormented like the prophets of old. Bare Your arm before these perverse men, and do not leave me for a moment. Today I ask this of You: pour the seven last plagues on anyone who dares to touch me!'*

"I don't know why, but I instinctively identified with you, with your case, and forgive me for daring to say it, but I wish I could have been like you. Ever since that moment, I have been hoping to have the opportunity to talk to you and make my confession, because I have decided to put an end to my life—it has no more meaning. In this place, I am the Lion! The Lion? Hardly! I am nothing but a monkey or a clown for them. I provide them with the entertainment of a fight whenever a poor wretch, condemned like me, thinks that by fighting he can gain esteem in the eyes of the others and perhaps gain some privileges. Being the strongest, hitting the hardest, beating an opponent, dominating others, at first gives you some pleasure, but as far as I'm concerned, I'm sick of it all. I've hit rock bottom!"

"Leonardo," I replied, "listen to me. Today salvation has come to this den! You can, just as you have done, unload your burden of anguish with me as a brother, if you so wish. I can help you reconcile with God through knowledge of His Word and in prayer. You don't need to confess your sins to me; I don't have the power to absolve you—no human has that power. It is to God alone that we must all confess our sins, small and great, and ask Him for His forgiveness."

"I don't think He can or, for that matter, wants to forgive me!" he answered. "I'm not even the shadow of the good person I was before that day when I had the encounter with that Russian. It's all been so terribly unfair, and I've been a horrible person!"

"Look," I said. "I cannot and will not justify your sins; sin is unjustifiable. But let's put it into perspective: In the first place, it is probable that you were dealt an injustice; there was probably an abuse of authority in condemning you to a place with so little possibility for survival. It appears to me that you were at the wrong place on the wrong day and with the wrong people. Then, when you arrived here, you definitely fell into the wrong place. No one should be here at the mercy of such corrupt people as these. But a mistake definitely occurred. Forgive me, but I'm not here to judge you; that is God's responsibility. But I do believe you urgently need help. You have to close certain chapters of your life: Regarding those who died, there is nothing you can do about it at this point. You need to let them go; leave that matter in God's hands. You need to get rid of hatred and resentment. Nor do I believe that remorse is the best way to find inner peace. For that reason, I want to speak to you about genuine repentance."

I paused for brief moment, so he could absorb the words I had spoken. I looked him in the eyes and continued. "The Bible offers the best medicine for what ails you: 'If we confess our sins, He is faithful and just to forgive us our sins and to cleanse us from all unrighteousness' [1 John 1:9]. This is a promise from God, and He does not lie. I see something very positive here; you wanted to confess your sins. There is another passage from the Bible that I want to share with you; I think this passage can work in your favor. Listen:

> "I acknowledged my sin to You,
> And my iniquity I have not hidden.
> I said, 'I will confess my transgressions to the LORD,'
> And You forgave the iniquity of my sin" (Psalm 32:5).

Tears welled up and began to pour from those eyes that once seemed so fierce. He looked at me and said with a broken voice, "Look! I'm crying; for years, I could not cry. My eyes seemed as hard as rock!"

I seized that moment to open before him the path of faith. That's when I called him brother for the first time, and he didn't resist: "Brother Leonardo, your tears reveal that the Holy Spirit has begun His work in your life!"

"Keep on talking to me, please," was all he could answer. He was convulsed with weeping.

So I continued, " 'Now I rejoice, not that you were made sorry, but that your sorrow led to repentance. For you were made sorry in a godly manner, that you might suffer loss from us in nothing. For godly sorrow produces repentance leading to salvation, not to be regretted; but the sorrow of the world produces death' " (2 Corinthians 7:9, 10).

These passages penetrated deep into the soul of that prisoner. The power of the Word of God is very great; it is like a two-edged sword. And the sword of God penetrates to the joints and marrow! It helped this desperate man to discern the intentions of his heart and the perfect will of God. Before that, I had seen many people react to the divine touch, but that night I had a much clearer picture of what the mercy of the Lord is like when working in favor of one who felt so unworthy. I am still amazed at the greatness, the depth, and the breadth of God's love.

Genuine repentance is not human fear of the consequences of our wrong deeds, nor is it the remorse felt by Judas, which led him to commit suicide. It is the pain we feel for having sinned in the first place; it is sadness for having done wrong; and it is an opening that allows desires for doing good to replace our hostile and perverse attitudes.

This is an experience that denotes a change of mind-set and produces a life change. Godly sorrow leads to repentance, to abandon sin, and, in its place, to develop a firm determination to take a stand, by the grace of God, against temptation that leads to sin.

"Let this truth enter into your head and make its nest in your breast!" I exclaimed to that convict. "No one has fallen so low that God's grace cannot lift him up; no one has gone so far that the love of God cannot reach him. Seize this hope! It will give you peace and comfort. You'll be a new person. God still loves you; He loves you like a parent loves a wayward child. Repent of your sins, and turn away from the wrong path. All of heaven is looking out for you; the angels are ready to come to your aid. As a result of your genuine repentance, there will be joy in heaven: 'I say to you that likewise there will be more joy in heaven over one sinner who repents than over ninety-nine just persons who need no repentance' " (Luke 15:7).

Dear reader, this is the Word of God. Jesus was crucified between two criminals. One of them, full of hatred and resentment, continued his cursing and recriminations; he does not seem to have repented but died a blasphemer. But the other repented and confessed his sins; Jesus granted him forgiveness and assurance of salvation.

When Zacchaeus, who was much more than an extortionist, an abuser, and a thief, confessed his sins and repented, Jesus said to him, "Today salvation has come to this house" (Luke 19:9).

That night I invited the Lion—the guy who killed Dracula—to kneel with me and repeat together a prayer of confession and repentance. He humbly knelt down. What a marvelous prayer that was! We both finished in tears, giving glory to God. And why deny it? In these moments as I write these lines, my eyes again are filled with tears of emotion and gratitude.

Leonardo was deeply touched and sincerely asked me, "Do you really believe that there is still a chance for me?"

I repeated, "No one is excluded from salvation. God's grace is sufficient for you and for me! God has received you today! And what you need is a new birth."

"A new birth? Tell me about it." But it was past midnight. I promised him that if I was allowed to return another day, I would do so. He called out to Hall to come and open the cell. The guard, puzzled at such a peaceful scene as I took my leave, took me back to my cell. Several brothers were awake and waiting for my return. They were happy and relieved that I was back safe and sound. But they could hardly believe it when I told them the story of all that had transpired: "The gospel has reached the man who killed Dracula."

1. Ellen G. White, *Prophets and Kings* (Nampa, ID: Pacific Press® Publishing Association, 2002), 479.

2. Ibid.

3. Ibid., 480.

4. Ibid., 539.

5. Ibid.

6. Ibid., 540.

7. See ibid., 540–542.

8. Ibid., 542.

9. Ibid., 543.

10. See ibid., 542, 543.

11. Ibid., 543, 544.

12. Ibid., 544.

Chapter 9

Conjugal Visit

Remove your way far from her, and do not go near the door of her house,
lest you give your honor to others, and your years to the cruel one.
—Proverbs 5:8, 9

That afternoon was full of strange foreboding for me. I felt the atmosphere to be very dense, and I was overwhelmed with an intense need to pray. So I did, even though I had no idea what was causing my stress. I spoke to the brothers about the importance of praying always and not to falter in this. At that moment, the prevailing silence and order were simply impressive.

I felt the presence of God in a very special way and invited the men to join me in a prayer session. Many of them still did not know yet what true prayer was.

"How can I truly pray?" asked Nicolas. "Old Slovasevich," he added, "laughed at those who prayed: Why do they need to ask God for something that He already knows to give? What are they going to tell God when He already knows everything? Besides, reciting prayers is like speaking to a figure made out of a piece of wood by someone cleverer than the next guy, just to make money. How can they pray to those figures they call saints if the figures can't hear, speak, feel, eat, or move around? And if they can't move, how can they help anyone?"

Some could repeat little memorized prayers common to many people, but they wondered if they had any special intercessory benefit. I taught them that prayer is the act of opening our hearts to God as to a friend. Following that, several of them dared to pray aloud in front of the others for the first time in their lives. I felt comforted and thanked God for the spiritual and social progress that my new brothers in the faith, as I called them, were making. At that hour, I was completely unaware of the trap that certain enemies were setting up for me shortly afterward, but soon it would unfold.

The guard in charge of a certain department entered the section, opened the door to the galley, and called out in a peculiar little voice: "Number one forty-four! Conjugal visit!" Everyone looked at me with surprise, and I felt confused. Knowing my wife well, I found it very strange that she had requested such a visit; it was impossible that she had been granted this visit. In addition, she was in an advanced state of pregnancy. Celita would then have been around eight months pregnant. Besides that, inmates in my unfavorable condition of confinement were not allowed such privileges. Something was very strange, it seemed to me; but the guard shook me out of my amazement, saying gruffly, "I can't stand here all afternoon. Start walking; she awaits!"

As we made our way through various corridors yet unknown to me, my mind was racing, trying to figure out what was going on. *How can this be if they haven't given me the privilege of normal visits? Why would they make an exception in my case? Is there a problem with my wife and child? What ploy might my wife have invented to get to see me?* But I found no logical answer to my questions.

At last, we came to a door that the guard opened and then said, "Enter, and wait inside." The room looked like something one might expect to find in a cheap motel. There was a nondescript bed, and the walls were entirely covered with mirrors. There was a bathroom, and another door leading to who knows where. They made me wait a long time; finally, the door opened and a girl came in, but she wasn't my wife. It was Margaret. Yes, I remembered her very well. She had been a classmate of mine from Mary of the Angels High School. She had been the star of the school gymnastics team in earlier times. She was the girl all the boys dreamed about, but none could ever conquer. She had a humble, sweet character and got along with everyone, but she was also decent, modest, and inaccessible. This seemed incredible. Was it a dream or a nightmare? Instinctively, I tried to escape, but the door was locked from the outside. Then she started talking to me in the same sweet voice I remembered from my days as a student. She called me by my last name, like everyone used to do at school: "I am here to help you. Come, let's talk."

I told her with a tone of disapproval, "I do not like this at all, Margaret. What are you doing here, and who set you up to do this?"

"Look, it may seem very strange that I am here, but really it isn't. I heard you were in trouble and decided to help. I work near where Captain Rosas works in the State Security Department, and he has authorized me to help resolve your situation. He arranged permission for this special conjugal visit, which is only awarded to very specific inmates, and it doesn't necessarily have to be with their wives. It will be completely confidential. I was totally honest with him when I told him that you always meant a lot to me. Do you understand me?"

I could not get over my disgust and replied, "Margaret, I don't understand what this is all about, and I'm very upset that you would put me in this situation. I should mean nothing to you! I'm a married man; I am also a pastor. All I ever felt for you was a normal classmate friendship, which it seems to me you are destroying by coming here in this unacceptable way."

She insisted, "I knew this would be your reaction; but I came to convince you, and I will insist until I succeed. I need to tell you something," she said. "If you don't understand, it probably is because you don't want to or maybe it is because of your silly religious notions. But we are now adults, and you have to know that you've always been the man of my dreams; and now, I will not miss my chance to be with you. I want to be near you and help you. Your wife does not have to know anything. I work undercover."

Having said that, she dropped her clothes and tried to embrace me; I did not expect such boldness and acknowledged that this was more difficult than having to deal with prisoners in the Lion's den. She was really a lioness! But God was stronger than the demons of sex, and I shouted in her face, "Get behind me, Satan! Do not touch me. Return to being the decent girl I remember from school! If your mother and your sisters could see what you are doing, they would die of shame." It didn't take much intelligence to realize that, whether she was telling the truth or not, Margaret was being used as a prostitute by the State Security in the service of the Communist government—she had become a miserable tool in their hands. To fall into that trap would have been the most shameful end I could have had.

I could not see my enemies, but I knew they were there. They laid in wait like hungry wolves seeking to devour my integrity, which was more precious to me than my own vital organs. They must have spied on me by some system, but I could not discover it; yet I knew with certainty that they were watching me and listening to my words. How shameful it was of them to practice these methods and try to morally destroy a man of God. And they claimed that it was their job to safeguard security; what shameless people! They will one day give an account of this when they stand before the judgment seat of God, which is coming soon.

What a hard experience that was! When you find yourself in a situation like the one I was in, being confined for so long, away from your wife, apparently all alone with such a beautiful creature, and in a private room—only God can set you free! The sex demons tried to overwhelm me. And I was battered with tempting advances. "Just do it; nobody will know. Don't be a fool and miss out!" But no, we must never forget that the devil is the devil. Honestly, I have to confess that at that moment all I could do was cry out, "Lord, have mercy on me!"

I never knew that Margaret worked for and had such close ties with the Communist government, and I never imagined that she had become such a hardened and aggressive woman with her sexuality. But there she was, ready for anything.

Seeing herself rejected, she began crying as she put her clothes back on and said, "I never thought this of you. I never thought you would refuse me. But here, I'll leave the name of a contact person." She put a business card on the bed, which I never picked up. "He works directly for Captain Rosas. If you decide to, he will come this very night and set you free. All you have to do is cooperate with him; he's a man of great authority and is a wonderful person. His department needs intelligent men like you—of your caliber. They have studied you well, and they know what they want. Everything can change for you today! And remember, I'll keep waiting for my chance to be with you. This situation must not end like this."

Later thanks to Sergeant G., I learned that all of this had indeed been a clever trap set up by three entities that failed: Margaret, with her double interest; the State Security Department, out to trip me up and destroy me; and my former colleague, who gave up being a minister, turned into a traitor, and offered the counsel of Balaam (see Numbers 25; 31:16). I learned that this former friend had been there with my enemies, watching the scene unfold from the next room through the mirror. He was waiting to celebrate my misfortune. But God was with me in His great might to defeat them!

The fear of God, which doesn't mean dread of God or apprehension, but rather fear of offending Him, helped me get through those difficult experiences. I often prayed, "Lord, never forget these terrible moments that they are putting me through. Forgive them, but keep my tears stored up as in a bottle!"

The fear of God is what gives us the wisdom, which we do not naturally possess, to differentiate between good and evil and to choose what is right. An irresponsible attitude on my part at that moment of temptation would have been a fatal blow to my young wife and to the future of my firstborn, who was soon to arrive. It would have also been disastrous for my youngest son who would eventually follow and for all my offspring through them who might not even have come to exist had I morally fallen that day. I am so very grateful for the blessed existence they now enjoy. Thank God for my family! He has given me much more than I could ever deserve!

The devil wants to destroy all those possibilities and blessings that God designs for our happiness. Satan rejoices when we take foolish steps in the wrong direction, blocking us from ever receiving the good things God wants to bring into reality in our lives.

His favorite activity remains to trick, seduce, and destroy the children of God. But God is in the business of teaching, converting, and redeeming His children who have fallen. He decided not to abandon us to our fate, whatever that might be. In this temptation that came to me, I could hear within my mind the unmistakable voice of Jesus saying, *"Remember My commandment: 'Thou shalt not commit adultery.' "* What a loving, tender, and compassionate God He is! He did not leave me in that moment of trial!

In God's great wisdom, He provided us with this shield of protection to spare us from having to live in pain and distress, darkness, and uncertainty. The ten great principles of God's government are expressed in the life and teachings of

Christ. These principles were written by the finger of God on two tablets of stone, and they are also written in our hearts when we accept Jesus as our Friend and Savior.

The Ten Commandments express the love, the will, and the purpose of God concerning human conduct and relationships and are binding upon all human beings in every age of history.

These precepts constitute the basis of the relationship God wishes to have with His children and the norm by which He will conduct the divine judgment, which we shall all face. Through the work of the Holy Spirit, these precepts unveil what is unacceptable in the sight of God, which is sin in all its manifestations. They teach us how to express love for God and human beings. They also make clear our inescapable need for a Savior.[1]

Salvation is by grace, not by works. Consider this simple spiritual formula:

$$S = GG + N.$$

Salvation is equal to God's Grace plus Nothing more, period.

It is the wonderful grace of God that saves us and redeems us; it opens before us the door to the kingdom of His love. Once we are saved, the Spirit begins to work within us, and that mysterious Power that convinces and converts will then transform us from glory to glory. We will then begin to love the spiritual things that we did not know before or perhaps even hated. We will also begin to dislike and turn away from the bad actions that we practiced before accepting Jesus.

Then appears the fruit of salvation, which in the first instance is obedience to the commandments. "This obedience develops Christian character and results in a sense of well-being. . . . The obedience of faith demonstrates the power of Christ to transform lives, and therefore strengthens Christian witness."[2]

When God gave the Ten Commandments on Mount Sinai, He revealed Himself as the Supreme Authority of the universe, but that was not all. He also revealed Himself as the Redeemer of His people. As He is the Savior, He called not only Israel but all of humanity to obey those ten brief but all-encompassing precepts: "Let us hear the conclusion of the whole matter: Fear God and keep His commandments, for this is man's all" (Ecclesiastes 12:13).

The Ten Commandments cover all the duties of humans toward God and toward other humans. If they were obeyed fully, we simply would not need so many law books to protect society. The law of God not only takes care of the institution of the family by warning against adultery but also covers all morality of humans. We can learn this in Exodus 20:3–17.

"You shall have no other gods before Me" (verse 3). The first commandment

was given to help us from falling into the illogical practice of revering fake or imaginative gods made in the image and likeness of the things different cultures consider remarkable. It warns us against polytheism, which is the belief in a multitude of gods and, of course, is a dangerous fallacy.

"You shall not make for yourself a carved image—any likeness; . . . you shall not bow down to them nor serve them" (verses 4, 5). The second commandment protects us from idolatry, which is the worship of false gods or false images of the true Divinity. This crude practice leads people to worship the stars, a stick of wood, stone carvings, animals, money, other humans, or the works of their hands. It is a sad insult to one's intelligence to worship anything other than the one Living God, the Creator of all things visible and invisible.

"You shall not take the name of the LORD your God in vain" (verse 7). The third commandment teaches us to respect God, because He is our Father, but also the only true God.

"Remember the Sabbath day, to keep it holy. Six days you shall labor and do all your work, but the seventh day is the Sabbath of the LORD your God" (verses 8–10). The fourth commandment requires us to sanctify the Sabbath. The Sabbath is an institution based on a period of time, twenty-four hours, which comes to us from a sinless world. It's like a special gift from the Creator that allows us to experience the reality of communion with Him. It also offers us the opportunity of physical rest, which is so necessary for our bodies and minds. God rested, not because He was tired or exhausted, but because He wanted to set an example for humans. He expects us to rest, sanctify the day, and worship Him.

"Honor your father and your mother, that your days may be long upon the land which the LORD your God is giving you" (verse 12). The fifth commandment exhorts us to honor our parents. It requires that we children submit to our parents as His agents assigned to transmit His will and family values on to future generations. We are to treat our parents with love and honor in all their dignity. This command includes a promise of longevity, which obviously also spans eternal life.

"You shall not murder" (verse 13). The sixth commandment prohibits murder. It was given to protect life, and it teaches us to consider life as sacred. We should not even wish death or evil to anyone with our thoughts. I thank God because I do not feel resentment toward those who did me wrong. I have forgiven my persecutors—those officials, for example, who ordered the police to search my home and confiscate my sermons typed out on an ancient Underwood typewriter. They said it was illegal reproduction of religious literature. Agents of the Communist government spied on me while I gave Bible studies, and of course, they took me away from my family and jailed me when I was trying to provide for my family and when I was carrying offerings to the denominational leaders. I simply leave these persecutors in the hands of the Almighty. God

says, "Beloved, do not avenge yourselves, but rather give place to wrath; for it is written, 'Vengeance is Mine, I will repay,' says the Lord" (Romans 12:19).

"You shall not commit adultery" (Exodus 20:14). The seventh commandment condemns adultery. Its main purpose is the protection of the family relationship; it prescribes purity of the marital relationship. In modern times, more than ever, it provides a safeguard against dangerous diseases of sexual transmission.

"You shall not steal" (verse 15). The eighth commandment condemns theft. It is a security fence around property. What a shame that in a supposedly highly developed civilization, we have to be protected by window bars, alarms, fences, and locks. If we all respected this commandment, what a free and pleasant life we could enjoy in our cities and in the countryside!

"You shall not bear false witness against your neighbor" (verse 16). The ninth commandment forbids slander, protects the truth, and condemns perjury. How much suffering and unnecessary distress are caused by slanderous persons! From the slanderer's mouth comes rotten lies that, when spread, stain innocent victims who have no way of defending themselves. The slanderer is usually a coward hiding in the shadows, who denies this vile action when confronted. Slander is even viler when it is directed against a family member or a friend; this is simply incomprehensible. Generally, the violation of this commandment is tied to another sin—jealousy, which eats away at the soul of the one who practices it. This is a sin against which no one can prevail; there is no way to protect oneself from envy. It's like a scorpion, which carries its poison inside. On the outside, the slanderer may appear to be an honest and spiritual person; but remember, one day the poison will kill him or her. At the final judgment, the slanderer will have to face the consequences of bearing false witness against his or her neighbor.

"You shall not covet your neighbor's house; you shall not covet your neighbor's wife, nor his male servant, nor his female servant, nor his ox, nor his donkey, nor anything that is your neighbor's" (verse 17). The tenth commandment condemns greed and reaches down to the root of all human relationships. It bans the greedy desire for what belongs to our neighbor.

The Ten Commandments have the special distinction of being the only words God spoke audibly to an entire nation. It is also the only portion of the Bible that God decided not to give by inspiration through a prophet but instead wrote out with His own finger and delivered to Moses to present to the people: "These words the LORD spoke to all your assembly, in the mountain from the midst of the fire, the cloud, and the thick darkness, with a loud voice; and He added no more. And He wrote them on two tablets of stone and gave them to me" (Deuteronomy 5:22).

"And when He had made an end of speaking with him on Mount Sinai, He gave Moses two tablets of the Testimony, tablets of stone, written with the finger of God" (Exodus 31:18).

"Jesus answered them, 'Most assuredly, I say to you, whoever commits sin is a slave of sin' " (John 8:34). When we do not obey the commandments of God's law, we are not free; obedience to the commandments assures us true freedom. Living within the protective boundaries of the will of God means freedom from sin. It also means being free of the trappings of sin: continuing concern, wounds to the conscience, and an increasing burden of guilt and remorse wearing down our vital strength. The psalmist says, "And I will walk at liberty, for I seek Your precepts" (Psalm 119:45).

We can all be free! It is not a complicated formula. Once saved by the blood of Christ, with His help we can live in harmony with the precepts of His kingdom—the Ten Commandments. "And you shall know the truth, and the truth shall make you free" (John 8:32)!

Even a prisoner can find freedom—freedom in Jesus—because that freedom transcends the walls and bars of any maximum-security prison.

---

1. See "The Law of God," Seventh-day Adventist Church, accessed September 7, 2016, https://www.adventist.org/en/beliefs/living/the-law-of-god/.

2. Ibid.

Chapter 10

The Fullness of Time

But when the fullness of the time had come, God sent forth His Son,
born of a woman, born under the law.

—Galatians 4:4

Every evening, after eating our rations, the small group of believers sat in the widest or least-congested part of the galley, right near the entry gate, and there we sang until guard Hall would order us to shut up. Other guards were more patient, and a few of them even drew close secretly and sang along from the outside. I taught the men a number of spiritual songs and hymns; but sometimes to confuse the enemy, we also sang a few folk songs until they got used to hearing our songs. I cannot but think that the providence of God protected us. Sergeant G. was instrumental in allowing us a degree of leeway so that our Bible studies could continue. Thankfully, the other guards kept their mouths shut and didn't turn us in for this activity. For some reason, one hymn especially impressed those men: "How Sweet Are the Tidings." I will say more about that later.

The next afternoon and for many evenings at about the same time, after the usual meeting with the group, Leonardo asked the guard to take me to his cell, and there we had a kind of secret Bible study. The "boss" did not want the others finding out that he was no longer the fierce Lion that he used to be. At that time, he was a little embarrassed, or perhaps nervous, about the possible reactions of his former supporters. Although we did not have a Bible, I presented to him what I had stored in my memory. Leonardo told me that he cupped his ears to listen to what we talked about in the galley during our meetings, and he also sang along with us.

One afternoon when I went to his cell, Leonardo said, "I have a surprise!"

I asked, "What is it?" And he brought out a Bible. I excitedly said, "This is wonderful! Where did you get it?"

He replied almost in a whisper, "I brought it in by the train."

"The train?"

"Look," he said, "this is a secret," and he showed me what he meant by the train. It was the most ingenious thing I could have imagined in prison. The idea behind it came from a prisoner who had been incarcerated at a very tough prison on the Isla de Pinos (known today as the Isle of Youth). "The train" consisted of a handwoven string made from unraveled socks. It took months of unstitching and unraveling enough socks. Some donated their socks for this purpose; others simply never knew how they went missing. Some inmates thought they disappeared by some feat of magic. The woven cord was very strong but thin and practically invisible. Leonardo's cell, like many others, had a window overlooking the courtyard of the prison. The simple system was designed for the transportation and communications of news, letters from friends, or to pass cigarettes, pornographic literature, and so on. It ended up being so effective that when the warden called for cell inspections to be carried out by the guards during the night, the alerted prisoners were able to move their precious objects from one extreme of the prison to the other without detection. Then the following night their things would be returned to them. The way it was established and worked was all a matter of ingenuity and patience. When the thin cord was ready and had enough length to reach twice the full length of the inner courtyard of the prison, one had to wait for a gusty day with the wind blowing in the right direction. Then a kind of kite was fashioned out of paper and flown to the desired location. There it would be grabbed by a cooperating inmate and passed around a window bar. Then the kite would send the remaining cord back to the cell it originated from, completing the loop. Things tied and suspended to that string could be pulled in one direction or the other. As this was several floors up and hard to see, it worked quite well for a long time without being discovered.

Grinning like a kid who had come up with a good prank, he continued, "I have a contact on the other side where there aren't so many restrictions. They go out to work repairing roads and highways, and they can get me things—like this Bible. It will cost me my fair share of cigarettes, but I think this is well worth it. I think it will be very useful to us. You can keep it with you, and when there is an inspection, you will know to get it to me to send by train to the other side. We will get it back afterward." To smuggle it over to my galley, I hid it on my back under my clothes where the waistband held it in place. How wonderful it was to have a Bible in my hands again. Just in case a guard might see it, I covered it with the end flaps of a novel by the Russian writer Leo Tolstoy, which someone had left in the bathroom. Thank God, they never discovered the hidden Bible. When I was finally released, Leonardo was able to keep it, and by then, he had learned to use it very well. I made him a series of Bible studies, connecting one text to another like a chain, so that he could more easily study the teachings of the Bible and various major Bible doctrines, such as the second coming of Christ, the signs of His coming, salvation, the state of the dead, and the sanctuary.

The members of the original group had begun to share their experiences of the last few weeks with the new inmates with whom we were placed in the second galley. I was glad to hear them talk about all the natural experiences as well as the supernatural ones, as they called them, from our so-called welcome cell. Some began to talk about changes in their lives. And I gave thanks to God again. The unintentional witnessing had started!

It is very difficult to feel the touch of God's love in our lives and not tell others about this great experience, even if you are a lifer.

Every day there were more who came to hear; some perhaps just out of curiosity, but others were experiencing a genuine transformation. Their vocabulary improved every day. These individuals no longer fought nor cursed; slowly they got rid of the ugly habit of calling each other by offensive and vulgar epithets and began calling themselves "brothers." That was the word I used when I addressed them in a respectful way. Something great and wonderful was starting to happen.

The previous day I had told them about the miraculous birth of Jesus, how He was born in Bethlehem of Judea, born of the virgin Mary by the intervention of the Holy Spirit. Through our study, many managed to understand that day what the work of a prophet is. I explained the meaning of the most important of all the Bible prophecies—that of the seventy weeks. It gives the exact time, with very clear and precise dates, when Jesus Christ was to appear on this earth. Daniel announced it five hundred years before it happened, and the prophecy was fulfilled in an accurate and extraordinary way.

Several of them expressed doubts and criticisms. Almansa raised his voice and said, "But how can it be possible that a man can announce something that will happen over five centuries later?" Then I shared with them, reading from my new Bible: "Of this salvation the prophets have inquired and searched carefully, who prophesied of the grace that would come to you, searching what, or what manner of time, the Spirit of Christ who was in them was indicating when He testified beforehand the sufferings of Christ and the glories that would follow" (1 Peter 1:10, 11).

"Daniel was a prophet; the Lord revealed to him what was going to happen. No human power can accurately predict the future. Only God knows that, because He sees the end from the beginning. There are false predictors and soothsayers who claim to know the future and deceive people for a short while, and some of their predictions stick; but their wiles and ruses are usually revealed. Only a true prophet can predict events years and even centuries before they occur and have these come true to the letter, because it is God who reveals them. We will submit this prophecy to the test, and if it fails, we will toss it out and abandon our claim that the Bible is the inspired Word of God. Does that sound reasonable to you?"

"Very good!" several of them replied.

Almansa, always more judicious, said, "Teacher, don't you think your statement is a little reckless? Would you really be willing to abandon the Bible if this prophecy turned out to be a fable like so many others?"

"Brother Almansa," I replied politely, "I know in whom I have believed. If I was not completely sure of my faith and my belief in the Bible as the sure Word of God, I would not be here today! I would not be a prisoner of conscience."

This understanding strengthened the faith of the new believers in Christ as the Divine Son of God and in the Bible, His Word. For many of the inhabitants of the Lion's den, the Bible was definitively confirmed as a reliable source that day, and it would become their rule of faith and practice. During the time yet remaining for us to study together, I was able to explain in great detail the exact fulfillment of these and other predictions of the prophet Daniel. I especially did my best to help them understand the ninth chapter of his book, which announced with astonishing accuracy the date when Jesus, the Messiah, would appear, bringing forgiveness and salvation to fallen humankind. This topic is important because if we believe in Jesus, if we accept Him as a Friend and Savior, we need to know all the evidence and be convinced that it is genuine.

They asked hundreds of other questions, some very good, which led me to speak more or less in terms similar to those expressed by the prophet:

Now while I was speaking, praying, and confessing my sin and the sin of my people Israel, and presenting my supplication before the LORD my God for the holy mountain of my God, yes, while I was speaking in prayer, the man Gabriel [the angel Gabriel], whom I had seen in the vision at the beginning, being caused to fly swiftly, reached me about the time of the evening offering. And he informed me, and talked with me, and said, "O Daniel, I have now come forth to give you skill to understand. At the beginning of your supplications the command went out, and I have come to tell you, for you are greatly beloved; therefore consider the matter, and understand the vision" (Daniel 9:20–23).

"Seventy weeks are determined
For your people and for your holy city,
To finish the transgression,
To make an end of sins,
To make reconciliation for iniquity,
To bring in everlasting righteousness,
To seal up vision and prophecy,
And to anoint the Most Holy.

"Know therefore and understand,
That from the going forth of the command

To restore and build Jerusalem
Until Messiah the Prince,
There shall be seven weeks and sixty-two weeks;
The street shall be built again, and the wall,
Even in troublesome times.

"And after the sixty-two weeks
Messiah shall be cut off, but not for Himself;
And the people of the prince who is to come
Shall destroy the city and the sanctuary.
The end of it shall be with a flood,
And till the end of the war desolations are determined.
Then he shall confirm a covenant with many for one week;
But in the middle of the week
He shall bring an end to sacrifice and offering.
And on the wing of abominations shall be one who makes desolate,
Even until the consummation, which is determined,
Is poured out on the desolate" (verses 24–27).

When you study this prophecy with a sincere heart and an open mind, it is difficult to deny that Jesus is the true Messiah: Five hundred years before Jesus' birth, Daniel predicts the year of Christ's baptism, the year of His crucifixion, and the year when the gospel would begin to be proclaimed to the world.

This prophecy also offers very powerful and convincing evidence that the Bible is no ordinary book but the Word of God.

Understanding the prophetic language

Because the seventy weeks are clearly a prophetic reckoning of time, they should be interpreted according to the principle of a day for a year, as stated in Ezekiel 4:6 and Numbers 14:34. On this basis, which is accepted by most scholars of prophecy, the 70 weeks equal—calculating 70 x 7 for the days in each week—490 days, or 490 years.

We need to identify the five major events mentioned in this prophecy:

1. A decree would be made to restore and rebuild Jerusalem, which was then in ruins.
2. It would be built again with plazas and walls.
3. At the end of that period, Messiah the Prince would come.
4. The life of the Messiah would be cut off "in the middle of the week."
5. The period of probation for the Jewish nation would end at the termination of the seventy prophetic weeks.

Secular history confirms this

Effectively, the order to rebuild Jerusalem was contained in the decree issued by King Artaxerxes of Media-Persia in 457 B.C., while confirming what two previous decrees issued by the kings Cyrus and Darius respectively had laid the groundwork for. The final form authorized the Jews to form their own government and empowered them to conduct worship in the city. In the first seven weeks, equal to forty-nine years (Daniel 9:25), the walls of the city were rebuilt, which began to take shape in the year 408 B.C.

Unto Messiah the Prince

It is very clear that the Messiah would appear on the stage of history at the end of the 69 weeks or after 483 years. Beginning that time calculation in 457 B.C., the date of the command to rebuild Jerusalem, leads us down to the year A.D. 27, the year in which Jesus was baptized by John the Baptist in the Jordan River and officially began His ministry. Notably, the Gospel of Luke says, "When all the people were baptized, it came to pass that Jesus also was baptized; and while He prayed, the heaven was opened. And the Holy Spirit descended in bodily form like a dove upon Him, and a voice came from heaven which said, 'You are My beloved Son; in You I am well pleased.' Now Jesus Himself began His ministry at about thirty years of age, being (as was supposed) the son of Joseph, the son of Heli" (Luke 3:21–23).

The story is beautiful and has no contradiction, despite the difference of three years, which you possibly have asked about: How can it be that Jesus was about thirty years old when He was baptized in the twenty-seventh year of His own era? The error is neither the Bible's nor that of prophecy, but that of the much later Dionysius Exiguus, when he produced his chronology. He made a mistake of three years in his calculation of the founding of Rome as it relates to the Christian era. Those three years lost in the tabulation were never clarified. That accounts for the fact that Jesus was *about* thirty years old when He was baptized in the year 27 of the Christian era.

Jesus carried out His public ministry during three and a half years—preaching, healing, doing good to those oppressed by the devil, and bringing liberty to the captives of sin.

It was prophesied that He would come to give His life as a ransom for many. His blood had to be shed, like the blood of a lamb—meek, pure, and unblemished—to pay the price for our sins.

Therefore, at the midpoint of the seventieth week, the Messiah's life was taken but not for Himself. The fact that Christ put an end to the "sacrifice and offering" offered in the earthly sanctuary makes it clear when He died and the veil in the temple was torn in two (Daniel 9:27).

Notice that Christ confirmed "a covenant with many for one week," or seven years, as predicted by Daniel (verse 27). He confirmed the covenant through His personal ministry for three and a half years and through the preaching of the apostles for three and a half years following that, which were dedicated to the Jewish nation.

But finally, in the year A.D. 34, the apostles began to take the gospel openly to other nations and peoples, thus ending the prophetic period of the seventy weeks.

In many ways, this period of 70 weeks, or 490 years, was the great climax of the centuries, which was longed for by patriarchs, prophets, and kings, and which was accomplished by the appearance, ministry, and atoning death of the Messiah.

The prophecies have been fulfilled:

- Jesus was born in Bethlehem (Matthew 2:1–6).
- He lived His life doing good deeds and healing all those oppressed by the devil (Mark 1:34).
- He died on the cross to save many (John 19:17–30).
- He rose on the third day (Luke 24:1–7).
- He ascended into heaven (Mark 16:19, 20).
- And He is now interceding for us in the heavenly sanctuary (Hebrews 8:1–6).

Everyone was amazed to learn that God's plan was fulfilled at the exact time He indicated; and just like the stars continue their steady course in the vast expanse, so God's plans know neither haste nor delay. As the apostle Paul told the believers in Galatia,

But when the fullness of the time had come, God sent forth His Son, born of a woman, born under the law, to redeem those who were under the law, that we might receive the adoption as sons.

And because you are sons, God has sent forth the Spirit of His Son into your hearts, crying out, "Abba, Father!" Therefore you are no longer a slave but a son, and if a son, then an heir of God through Christ (Galatians 4:4–7).

Understanding these truths was so significant for these prisoners and so precious to their captive souls that many of them repeated continuously, and others joined in shouting: "I'm free! I'm free! I'm free in Jesus Christ!" Such was the impact on the prison population that there was great contention and much criticism. Those who did not understand the concept of freedom in the Spirit accused the believers of being crazy. So that day it became necessary to conduct an additional study to help harmonize this spiritual knowledge and the actual reality of each individual. That midmorning session, rather than a religious meeting, seemed almost like a riot.

Pedro Malagón, a heavyset, dark-skinned man serving a life sentence, shouted out in his frustration, "I had a Jesus [figurine]! It was a nice one, made of bronze, and I always kept it hanging in the cab of my truck. But on the day of my accident, it did nothing for me. That Jesus couldn't help me! It did not prevent me from doing the brutal thing I did." I later learned that Malagón, while driving a huge Soviet-built KP3 truck, had rammed it as fast as possible and with evil intention into a group of five people, in an attempt to kill the chief of his work brigade because of some differences related to participation in the microbrigades.

These microbrigades were groups formed to build apartments that, once completed, were allocated as low-income rentals to participants by turn; but this benefit was only open to those privileged to be accepted into the plan. The criteria for participation in the microbrigades were based on merit earned by the employee, such as putting in many hours of "voluntary" work and, above all else, showing a correct political attitude. It was a long process, representing much personal sacrifice and many months of required work without pay, but it was the only hope for many workers to get a rental unit.

Malagón had been living in a common room without a private bathroom, along with his wife and four children, for almost ten years. Due to the ongoing housing crisis that Cuba suffers, they had no opportunity to live as a family in a single-family home or even in a decent apartment. He excused his violent crime by saying that this fellow, the head of personnel, played dirty by preventing him from participating in the plan that would entitle him to rent the dreamed-for apartment. This boss, he swore, had given a "less deserving" worker that opportunity just because he was his relative.

Then on that fateful day, seeing his hated boss among the group there in the baseball stadium they were building, he seized the moment to brutally run him over without even stopping to think about the other coworkers who had nothing to do with his problem. He got his revenge, but the attack killed three of the five persons he struck; of the remaining two, one was left paralyzed, and the other suffered serious injuries.

It was really hard to see that hulk of a man crying like a child over his situation and blaming his bronze Jesus for it all: "What freedom can He give me now? That day my Jesus just hung there, staring out but not seeing me." The angry inmate stood poised in stiff defiance. "If only He had turned the wheel at that moment and the truck had gone six feet off course, nothing would have happened! I wouldn't be here. I don't believe in Jesus anymore, and I don't believe in anything!"

Brother Gravarán tried to clarify things for his fellow prisoner in a fraternal spirit, which moved me greatly: "Make no mistake, Malagón, I used to think the same as you. I believed that God, Jesus, and the virgin were those figures that my mother had hanging on the wall; but now I understand that these images can't eat, drink, or smell, and they sure don't think. They are just that—images. I've learned that God is real, He is Spirit, and that we must worship Him in spirit and in truth. It's the same as this picture that I have here of my mom. If I ask the photo to give me lunch, nothing happens; but if I could ask my mother in person right now, she would fix me a banquet. Keep in mind that those images supposedly of God are not real likenesses of Him because no one has seen Him. There are no true images of Jesus or the virgin either. You are the only one responsible for what you did, not some dangling Jesus doll in your truck. You need to go to the real Jesus in spirit and ask Him to take away your guilt and to forgive you. He is alive and will do that for you, but not some doll made by an artisan who is just another man like yourself."

Motivated by what was happening, I spoke to them again at length about Jesus, more or less in these terms: "Listen, Brothers, be at peace, and listen to what I have to say. God had spoken to humans for centuries—ever since our first parents, Adam and Eve, fell into sin—through nature, by means of figures and symbols, and by the voice of patriarchs and prophets. But when the time was right, the great historical moment, when Divine Omniscience knew it was time, God manifested Himself in human flesh. It was necessary that He come to this world and be made a man like one of us but without ceasing to be God. When the known world was under one government, the Roman Empire, when there was a common language recognized as the literary language of the age, and when roads were being built to reach the most remote places, all of this came together to prepare the world for the rapid spread of knowledge concerning the Savior of humankind. I'm sure God marshaled many other factors, some of which are yet unknown to us, when He made the determination to send His Son to our world. He knew what He was doing when He said, 'Now!' And Christ, His eternal Son, was willing to volunteer for the dreadful sacrifice in order to rescue fallen humanity."

Was Jesus God?

"Teacher," Brother Almansa said, "something seems contradictory about Jesus. You say He was born of the virgin Mary and that He is God. But how is it possible that God could be the Son of a Jewish peasant, who must have lived about four thousand years after God created Adam and obviously the same four thousand years before Mary was born?"

"Very good question, Brother Almansa," I replied. "We need to understand that when we talk about Jesus Christ, we are not talking about a man who tried to become God. When we talk of Christ, the Messiah, we are talking about God, the Eternal God and Creator who decided to become a man in order to save humankind from eternal death, the result of the fall into sin. Remember this well: the story of Jesus is not the story of a man who wanted to become God. It is the story of God who decided to become man—Jesus Christ who was, is, and forever remains God! He came to earth and took human nature; He was made a man so He could save us! Throughout the universe, there is no one else like Him: God and yet truly man!"

Godofredo then spoke up, "I understand, Teacher! The point is that Jesus Christ was something like half God and half man."

"No, my dear Brother Godofredo. Jesus Christ was and is one hundred percent God and came also to be one hundred percent man. He is not half God and half man. He is fully God, just as God the Father, and fully man just like you and me. This act of God's love is something supernatural. It is the essence of a great mystery, which we will be learning about during eternity; it is the mystery of godliness:

"And without controversy great is the mystery of godliness:

"God was manifested in the flesh,
Justified in the Spirit,
Seen by angels,
Preached among the Gentiles,
Believed on in the world,
Received up to glory (1 Timothy 3:16).

Jesus has been through the endless ages: Magnificent and Invincible, Faithful Teacher, Eternal Creator, Almighty God of universal harmony.

"At the very beginning of the Gospel of John, the apostle declares by divine inspiration that God the Son is coeternal with the Father: 'In the beginning was the Word, and the Word was with God, and the Word was God. He was in the beginning with God. All things were made through Him, and without Him nothing was made that was made. In Him was life, and the life was the light of men' [John 1:1–4].

"Sin had separated Adam and Eve from the Source of life and potentially should have caused their immediate death. But God the Son stepped between them and divine justice, bridging the gap, thus preventing their death at that moment. Even before the Cross, grace kept sinners alive and assured them salvation; but in order for them to be fully restored as sons and daughters of God, He had to become a man. This sublime act of mercy was carried out, not because the Deity needed it in any way, but for the sake of humanity, which had deviated from the path of righteousness. I sum it up in this way: the supreme work of the Creator was that He became the Savior of the work of His own hands.

"Because of sin, which is defined as the transgression of the law of God, the human race was in danger of eternal death. The law of God demanded the life of the sinner. But by His infinite love, God gave His Son as a substitute and surety: 'For God so loved the world that He gave His only begotten Son, that whoever believes in Him should not perish but have everlasting life' [John 3:16].

"The prophet Isaiah foretold that the Savior would come as a male child and would be both human and divine:

"For unto us a Child is born,
Unto us a Son is given;
And the government will be upon His shoulder.
And His name will be called
Wonderful, Counselor, Mighty God,
Everlasting Father, Prince of Peace [Isaiah 9:6].

"The place of His birth was also foretold by the prophet Micah:

"But you, Bethlehem Ephrathah,
Though you are little among the thousands of Judah,
Yet out of you shall come forth to Me
The One to be Ruler in Israel [Micah 5:2].

"The birth of this divine-human person would be supernatural. Referring to the predictions of the prophet Isaiah [Isaiah 7:14], the evangelist Matthew says, ' "Behold, the virgin shall be with child, and bear a Son, and they shall call His name Immanuel," which is translated, "God with us" ' [Matthew 1:23].

"The mission of the Savior is expressed in the following words:

"The Spirit of the LORD is upon Me,
Because He has anointed Me
To preach the gospel to the poor;
He has sent Me to heal the brokenhearted,
To proclaim liberty to the captives
And recovery of sight to the blind,
To set at liberty those who are oppressed" (Luke 4:18).

Then I declared with enthusiasm and energy, "Yes, my brothers, this is understood spiritually; but it means freedom for the captives and the opening of the prison. Because no matter that we're here, we can be free in Christ, free from our guilt, free from our past sins, free to love God, free to love our families even when they are far away, and free to love our neighbors." So enthused were the prisoners that they started clapping.

"Please don't applaud me," I requested.

Gravarán shouted out, "It's not you, Teacher; it is what you just said!" And they applauded all the more. I also joined in giving a hand to God for all the good He has done for me and the great sacrifice His Son made to save us.

I concluded, "How incomprehensible is His condescension toward us! God the eternal Son paid the price Himself and bore the punishment for all the crimes and sins committed by everyone in this prison, as well as in all the other prisons in the world and for every sinner throughout history and around the world, right down to you and me."

Then I asked all those who accepted Christ as their personal Friend, Lord, and Savior to kneel down to pray and commit their souls to follow Jesus, whatever the cost. About fifteen covenanted with God that afternoon. Jesus' name was mentioned in every corner of the galley; for many of the prisoners, it was a subject of joy. Salvation had come to this dreary place, and praises were heard over the curses and oaths of others. I must also recognize that the name of Jesus became the cause of dissension, many discussions, and endless debates. The wave produced by the good news of the gospel somehow spread to other galleys and cells. The discussions were primarily with atheists and spiritualists. Because of the kind of convicts who formed the population of the Lion's den—almost 100 percent of them were there for violent crimes or other horrible perversions—very few of them had ever been part of any Christian or evangelical church. Almost all of those who accepted Christ were doing so for the first time and had never before been exposed to the preaching of the gospel.

Then I understood more clearly why it was necessary that someone had to unjustly pass through the valley of the shadow of death. I was confirmed in my conviction that God has a plan to make Himself known to humans, even when they find themselves in the most desperate of conditions. His loving and powerful hand reaches across the chasm of anguish and pain. There is hope for everyone! You, dear reader, if you find yourself in difficult times, *never lose hope!* God still has the same power as ever to work wonders, transform lives, and provide for our needs.

I invite you right now to kneel down to pray and talk to the Lord. Give glory to God and surrender to Him, placing your problems, your concerns, and your life at His feet. He will not reject or leave you out, because He says, "The one who comes to Me I will by no means cast out" (John 6:37).

If you are already a mature, faithful Christian, renew your covenant to always walk with Jesus. If you are facing difficulties, He has solutions for you: Be free in Christ! Take hold of faith! Never lose hope!

Chapter 11

The Blessed Hope!

*Looking for the blessed hope and glorious appearing
of our great God and Savior Jesus Christ.*

—Titus 2:13

Coming to understand the historical reality of Christ—that Jesus was and is a real person, a historical character, and that all the prophetic-historical data related to Him is true—opened the minds and hearts of my fellow prisoners like nothing else could. Their appetite for spiritual things was evident. They were full of expectations and excitement. As with one voice, they insisted, "Tell us, Teacher, what comes next? Is that the end of it all? What else can we expect?"

"No, Brothers, that is not the end of it! We still lack the most important part. Jesus is coming again!"

I opened the Bible, this time to the Gospel of John, and read for them this passage full of joyful hope: "Let not your heart be troubled; you believe in God, believe also in Me. In My Father's house are many mansions; if it were not so, I would have told you. I go to prepare a place for you. And if I go and prepare a place for you, I will come again and receive you to Myself; that where I am, there you may be also" (John 14:1–3).

His first coming gives us assurance that He will come again

Before ascending to heaven, Jesus Himself gave us this promise through His disciples, and I firmly believe that the greatest assurance we have for believing in His second coming is the fact of His first coming. Jesus guaranteed this by His personal promise when He said, "I will come again." He already came once, and now He is preparing to return a second time to take us home with Him.

The excitement was overwhelming; the prisoners were like children receiving a new toy. In none of the major evangelistic campaigns I had previously conducted had I ever seen such spontaneous rejoicing when sharing this, the greatest Bible teaching, which is the blessed hope of Jesus' return. *So this means that there is hope for me, that my life will not end forever in this filthy prison!"* Full of conviction, I repeated to them, "Jesus is coming a second time! He is coming to find us! We can be very sure of the Second Coming! The first coming of the Messiah gives us great certainty that the Second Coming will take place."

We read in the Acts of the Apostles what happened on the very day that Jesus ascended to heaven in the presence of His disciples and what the angels said in confirmation of His return. Jesus had just given them the Great Commission to go and share His testimony with all nations, beginning first in Judea and Samaria. He promised that they would receive the baptism of the Holy Spirit to empower their work on earth. After those testimonies and promises, He ascended to heaven to carry out the heavenly sanctuary intercession for us. His departure is recorded in these words: "Now when He had spoken these things, while they watched, He was taken up, and a cloud received Him out of their sight. And while they looked steadfastly toward heaven as He went up, behold, two men stood by them in white apparel, who also said, 'Men of Galilee, why do you stand gazing up into heaven? This same Jesus, who was taken up from you into heaven, will so come in like manner as you saw Him go into heaven' " (Acts 1:9–11).

There can be no doubt about it, Heaven's plan is clear: the same Jesus who was born in a stable in Bethlehem of Judea; the same Jesus who went about preaching and doing good to those afflicted by the devil; the same Jesus who was crucified on the cross of Calvary, who came back to life on the third day, and who ascended into heaven; that very same Jesus will return for a second time but without any further subjection to death and the grave, because He already gained that victory. He is now coming for His children as promised. What a beautiful confirmation of Jesus' promise those angels spoke! And when this all unfolds, it will be public and visible: "Behold, He is coming with clouds, and every eye will see Him, even they who pierced Him. And all the tribes of the earth will mourn because of Him. Even so, Amen" (Revelation 1:7).

He will come in the same way as the disciples saw Him go to heaven. His second coming will not be hidden from the eyes of the people; it will be seen by all the inhabitants of the earth. The Bible emphasizes this truth that the Lord will appear openly and visibly when He returns for the second time: "Looking for the blessed hope and glorious appearing of our great God and Savior Jesus Christ" (Titus 2:13).

Then I paraphrased for the prisoners a portion of text that I knew very well, almost from memory.

It is at midnight that God manifests His power for the deliverance of His people. The sun appears, shining in its strength. Signs and wonders follow in quick succession. The wicked look with terror and amazement upon the scene, while the righteous behold with solemn joy the tokens of their deliverance. Everything in nature seems turned out of its course. The streams cease to flow. Dark, heavy clouds come up and clash against each other. In the midst of the angry heavens is one clear space of indescribable glory, whence comes the voice of God like the sound of many waters, saying: "It is done." Revelation 16:17.

That voice shakes the heavens and the earth. There is a mighty earthquake, "such as was not since men were upon the earth, so mighty an earthquake, and so great." Verses 17, 18. The firmament appears to open and shut. The glory from the throne of God seems flashing through. The mountains shake like a reed in the wind, and ragged rocks are scattered on every side. There is a roar as of a coming tempest. The sea is lashed into fury. There is heard the shriek of a hurricane like the voice of demons upon a mission of destruction. The whole earth heaves and swells like the waves of the sea. Its surface is breaking up. Its very foundations seem to be giving way. Mountain chains are sinking. Inhabited islands disappear. The seaports that have become like Sodom for wickedness are swallowed up by the angry waters. Babylon the great has come in remembrance before God, "to give unto her the cup of the wine of the fierceness of His wrath." Great hailstones, every one "about the weight of a talent," are doing their work of destruction. Verses 19, 21. The proudest cities of the earth are laid low. The lordly palaces, upon which the world's great men have lavished their wealth in order to glorify themselves, are crumbling to ruin before their eyes. Prison walls are rent asunder, and God's people, who have been held in bondage for their faith, are set free.

Graves are opened, and "many of them that sleep in the dust of the earth . . . awake, some to everlasting life, and some to shame and everlasting contempt." Daniel 12:2. . . .

. . . Fierce lightnings leap from the heavens, enveloping the earth in a sheet of flame. Above the terrific roar of thunder, voices, mysterious and awful, declare the doom of the wicked. The words spoken are not comprehended by all; but they are distinctly understood by the false teachers. Those who a little before were so reckless, so boastful and defiant, so exultant in their cruelty to God's commandment-keeping people, are now overwhelmed with consternation and shuddering in fear. Their wails are heard above the sound of the elements. Demons acknowledge the deity of Christ and tremble before His power, while men are supplicating for mercy and groveling in abject terror.

. . . Those who have sacrificed all for Christ are now secure, hidden as in the secret of the Lord's pavilion. They have been tested, and before the world and the despisers of truth they have evinced their fidelity to Him who died for them. A marvelous change has come over those who have held fast their integrity in the very face of death. They have been suddenly delivered from the dark and terrible tyranny of men transformed to demons. Their faces, so lately pale, anxious, and haggard, are now aglow with wonder, faith, and love. . . .

Soon there appears in the east a small black cloud, about half the size of a man's hand. It is the cloud which surrounds the Saviour and which seems in the distance to be shrouded in darkness. The people of God know this to be the sign of the Son of man. In solemn silence they gaze upon it as it draws nearer the earth, becoming lighter and more glorious, until it is a great white cloud, its base a glory like consuming fire, and above it the rainbow of the covenant. Jesus rides forth as a mighty conqueror. Not now a "Man of Sorrows," to drink the bitter cup of shame and woe, He comes, victor in heaven and earth, to judge the living and the dead. "Faithful and True," "in righteousness He doth judge and make war." And "the armies which were in heaven" (Revelation 19:11, 14) follow Him. With anthems of celestial melody the holy angels, a vast, unnumbered throng, attend Him on His way. The firmament seems filled with radiant forms—"ten thousand times ten thousand, and thousands of thousands." No human pen can portray the scene; no mortal mind is adequate to conceive its splendor. "His glory covered the heavens, and the earth was full of His praise. And His brightness was as the light." Habakkuk 3:3, 4. As the living cloud comes still nearer, every eye beholds the Prince of life. No crown of thorns now mars that sacred head; but a diadem of glory rests on His holy brow. His countenance outshines the dazzling brightness of the noonday sun. "And He hath on His vesture and on His thigh a name written, *King of kings, and Lord of lords.*" Revelation 19:16. . . .

Amid the reeling of the earth, the flash of lightning, and the roar of thunder, the voice of the Son of God calls forth the sleeping saints. He looks upon the graves of the righteous, then, raising His hands to heaven, He cries: "Awake, awake, awake, ye that sleep in the dust, and arise!" Throughout the length and breadth of the earth the dead shall hear that voice, and they that hear shall live. And the whole earth shall ring with the tread of the exceeding great army of every nation, kindred, tongue, and people. From the prison house of death they come, clothed with immortal glory, crying: "O death, where is thy sting? O grave, where is thy victory?" 1 Corinthians 15:55. And the living righteous and the risen saints unite their voices in a long, glad shout of victory. . . .

The living righteous are changed "in a moment, in the twinkling of an eye." At the voice of God they were glorified; now they are made immortal and with the risen saints are caught up to meet their Lord in the air. Angels "gather together His elect from the four winds, from one end of heaven to the other." Little children are borne by holy angels to their mothers' arms. Friends long separated by death are united, nevermore to part, and with songs of gladness ascend together to the City of God.

On each side of the cloudy chariot are wings, and beneath it are living wheels; and as the chariot rolls upward, the wheels cry, "Holy," and the wings, as they move, cry, "Holy," and the retinue of angels cry, "Holy, holy, holy, Lord God Almighty." And the redeemed shout, "Alleluia!" as the chariot moves onward toward the New Jerusalem.[1]

All the prisoners in our galley were there; their faces were radiant; and many wept without reservation. Some of them repeated, "Holy, holy, holy!" Others exclaimed, "Hallelujah!" Some said, "Thank You, Lord, for allowing us to know these wonders!"

Then I said, "Everyone turn to a brother near you and shake his hand then repeat, 'Christ is coming soon!' "

I started singing our hymn, "How Sweet Are the Tidings," and everyone joined in:

How sweet are the tidings that greet the pilgrim's ear,
As he wanders in exile from home!
Soon, soon will the Savior in glory appear,
And soon will the kingdom come.

Refrain
He's coming, coming, coming soon I know,
Coming back to this earth again;
And the weary pilgrims will to glory go,
When the Savior comes to reign.

The mossy old graves where the pilgrims sleep
Shall be open as wide as before,
And the millions that sleep in the mighty deep
Shall live on this earth once more.

There we'll meet ne'er to part in our happy Eden home,
Sweet songs of redemption we'll sing;
From the north, from the south, all the ransomed shall come,
And worship our heavenly King.

Hallelujah, Amen! Hallelujah again!
Soon, if faithful, we all shall be there;

O, be watchful, be hopeful, be joyful till then,
And a crown of bright glory we'll wear.[2]

We felt God's presence like never before! It was a moment I will never forget! I await that glorious day of the Second Coming so that I can see my parents and grandparents again, all my loved ones who rest in the grave, and those at present whom I cannot see because circumstances separate us. But in a very special way, I look forward to that glorious day of Christ's second coming, so I can be reunited again with my brothers in prison—those who came to know Jesus in such oppressive circumstances and those who found the path of salvation through their subsequent ministry.

---

1. Ellen G. White, *The Great Controversy* (Nampa, ID: Pacific Press® Publishing Association, 2002), 636–641, 644, 645.

2. "How Sweet Are the Tidings," in *The Seventh-day Adventist Hymnal* (Hagerstown, MD: Review and Herald® Publishing Association, 1985), hymn no. 442.

Chapter 12

Of Water and the Spirit

Jesus answered, "Most assuredly, I say to you, unless one is born of water and the Spirit, he cannot enter the kingdom of God."

—John 3:5

That afternoon Sergeant G., the head of operations, gave orders for me to be brought for a work detail moving some furniture and files in his office. He looked for tasks like that when he wanted to talk to me about something personal without anyone catching on. As he said, we must make sure "the coast is clear."

"Son," he said, "I have good news and bad news for you." I began to feel uneasy. But he continued, "The good news is that you are going to get out of the Lion's den and will be moved to the penal farm; although you'll have to work very hard, at least you'll be outdoors in the sunlight, and the food is a little better. The inmate population on the farm is very different because out there in that world you will be with the political prisoners. They are mostly decent people, a fact that displeases some of our leaders. They do not fight each other, and hardly anything is lost. They aren't thieves in that area, but they are the worst enemies of the revolution and are the most closely watched. Do not think that you will be going there because of good behavior or anything like that. What is happening is that some informants have reported that you are corrupting the prisoners with religious ideas, which is considered 'ideological diversionism.' Nobody has been found to accuse you directly, because here in the Lion's den being considered a snitch could cost a guy his life, and it isn't worth losing an informant over a problem like yours.

"Now you need to know that when they move you out among the political prisoners, you will be all the more in the crosshairs because there are certain ones planted there who aren't really what they appear to be. They are undercover agents who are responsible for closely monitoring any activity, and they are very skilled; none of us—not even I—know who they are. The prison commissioner and the reeducation officer realize that they have been unable to break you under the harsh conditions of the Lion's den, and this they cannot forgive, so they have come up with this new strategy. You are to be considered a counter-revolutionist just pretending to be a humble religious person; they will be looking for the opportunity to catch you proselytizing and speaking ill of the revolution, which will net you a stiff sentence. They would like to see you get at least twenty years. I don't know your transfer date yet; but it will be soon because they are eager to start the new tactic."

I thanked Sergeant G. and prayed for him. I also realized clearly that I had to hurry my work on behalf of my prison brothers. How incredible it seemed, but obviously some of the convicts, who were hardened criminals, were also supporters of the Communist ideology and were prepared to hinder the work of preaching the gospel. Who knows how, but they obviously had their way of passing information to the reeducator. Here I was, once again being denounced, but this time from inside the prison, accused of corrupting the prisoners by my spiritual witnessing, just as I had been accused of doing on the outside among the general population. Interestingly enough, it was not the hall guards who denounced me; at times, they had tried to hush our singing but nothing more. I never knew the reason for their discretion. Someone commented that possibly it was because our religious work produced a more wholesome environment with fewer problems and less work for them. In any case, God bless them for this tolerant attitude.

On my part, it seemed best to make no comment; but in my thoughts and heart, it was clear what must be done. I had never been in a situation quite like this; it was urgently important to leave the new believers well organized, otherwise everything would end up having been just a passing phenomenon, and definitely that was not the objective. That night the once fearsome Leonardo, "the man who killed Dracula," came to the meeting; the brothers were happy to see him there, singing and humbly adding his amens. The topic that night was a very important one, I announced; it was about the "new birth." After singing several hymns I had taught them, we prayed and opened the Bible to the Gospel of John, chapter 3:

> There was a man of the Pharisees named Nicodemus, a ruler of the Jews. This man came to Jesus by night and said to Him, "Rabbi, we know that You are a teacher come from God; for no one can do these signs that You do unless God is with him."
>
> Jesus answered and said to him, "Most assuredly, I say to you, unless one is born again, he cannot see the kingdom of God."
>
> Nicodemus said to Him, "How can a man be born when he is old? Can he enter a second time into his mother's womb and be born?"
>
> Jesus answered, "Most assuredly, I say to you, unless one is born of water and the Spirit, he cannot enter the kingdom of God" (John 3:1–5).

At that moment, Leonardo spoke up: "Teacher, I already know what this is about." Everyone present was amazed to hear him speak in those terms. The inmate brothers could not believe their ears. But he, realizing the strange impression his words were making, continued on with his declaration that went more or less like this: "Brothers, it has been very difficult to bring myself to say what I say today in the presence of many of you who know my past life and part of my story here. I have been a child of the devil, an abuser, a murderer, and the most miserable person in the world. 'The man who killed Dracula,' as everyone hisses between their teeth! But what none of you know is that I wanted to die and could not, and I went through horrible anguish that felt like a rat eating my heart out day and night. But it never ended, and I lived on with that terrible pain. Then, in recent weeks, God has visited me. And I died. Yes! The Lion, the man who killed Dracula, is dead! He died a murderer! But I am born again! Today I declare this before you all as a child of God, and I want to apologize to all those I have hurt and abused," and he started naming names and confessing his sins one by one. "Today I recognize the magnitude of my decision," he went on, "I know the risks I run for making this promise to the Lord that my hands will no longer kill or destroy. But I accept everything for the love of my Jesus, whose hands were nailed for me on the cross of Calvary! I was born of the Spirit, and now I want to be born of water! Please, baptize me, Pastor!" He took off his hat and showed us that he had cut his lionlike mane, a symbol of his past life. "I want to be baptized now!"

"Brother Leonardo," I said, "I thank God for your decision. But to baptize you, we are going to need water, lots of water, and not just a few drops on your head. Remember that Jesus was baptized by John the Baptist in the Jordan River. For biblical baptism, it is necessary to be immersed completely as a symbol of death and burial to sin and then come up out of the water into perfect rebirth as a new creature."

I felt very moved and thankful, as I was about to leave the Lion's den and my ministry for them was soon to end. How wonderful that in just a few months God had formed a group of believers in the worst and most difficult place possible, and now He was raising up a preacher—coarse and brutal, if you care to think that—but the ideal one to guide those inmates on the difficult path that yet stretched out before them until the Great Day of Liberation would finally arrive.

Then Brother Gravarán said, "Teacher! There is a water tank in the bathroom. It's like a big barrel, which is always kept full for times of emergency or in the event of fire. Would it be enough? Can we consider this an emergency?"

I replied joyfully, "Of course! I think that a barrel is enough if we are creative. And yes, this is a case of emergency and of fire. Because the fire of the Holy Spirit is working and purifying hearts here tonight!

"Brothers, is there anyone else who wants to make his covenant with God tonight through baptism? Come and let us have prayer asking the Father to baptize you with the Spirit, and I will baptize you with water." Then one by one, sixteen prisoners made their decision.

After that precious moment of prayer, we went to the bathroom area; the barrel was full, and I began the strangest baptismal ceremony of my life. It was unconventional as I could not tilt the candidates back, but they had to squat down under the water after I offered for each a personal baptismal declaration similar to this: "My dear brother Leonardo, because you have accepted Jesus as your personal Savior, because you have decided to follow Christ as the new Leader of your life, and because you have decided to leave your old ways behind, now, for the forgiveness of your sins and the beginning of a new life in Christ, as a minister of the gospel I baptize you in the name of the Father, the Son, and the Holy Spirit! Amen!"

That memorable night seventeen precious souls were baptized; Brother Malagón decided to join the other sixteen as we were completing the service. He didn't think he could fit into the barrel; but with the help of Gravarán and others, we got him in, so he, too, was baptized. There was much joy in heaven that night! For I say unto you, there is more joy in heaven over one inmate who repents than over ninety-nine people on the outside who think they are good enough already (see Luke 15:7)!

The underground church

The next two and a half days were spent working out a structured plan for the new group of baptized Christians so that they could function in an orderly way. It was simple but strong enough to maintain the unity and integrity of their small church. I had no experience in such situations, and those new brothers even less. So praying and applying biblical concepts as well as adaptations from the regular church outside of prison, we came up with an arrangement that looked promising for the prison church.

Maybe it was not a completely orthodox system; but it was biblical, and it has continued to work, as I read in the yellowed pages that later reached me.

This is what we came up with:

1. We appointed several leaders for the newborn church.
   a. An elder or spiritual leader who would take care of preaching and teaching. That responsibility fell on none other than Leonardo, the man who killed Dracula.
   b. A deacon who is responsible for organizing meetings, finding and preparing the place and occasion. Gravarán was chosen for this responsibility.
2. I explained how each one could work together as part of the body of Christ, the church.

3. I taught them how to arrive at decisions and show mutual respect within the group.
4. I reinforced the main points of doctrine.
5. We returned the underlined Bible to Leonardo with many major texts indicated to support each fundamental doctrine.
6. We wrote out the lyrics to all the hymns I could remember.

The next day there came a very difficult and emotional time; I can never forget the voice of the guard who came to move me to the farm where political prisoners were held. He shouted out, "One forty-four, collect your belongings, you are being transferred!"

While collecting my few belongings, the prison brothers came and tearfully hugged me and said Goodbye. It was a very hard moment, in all honesty—so difficult and not at all easy. Yes, I was leaving the Lion's den and going out to see the light of day once again, but I was leaving behind the first fruits of my work and suffering there in that dismal prison.

When the gate opened, I said, "Brothers, we will see each other again on that great day that is soon to come! I commend you to the grace of God and the ministry of the Holy Spirit."

The guard stopped me: "There is no time for little speeches; there is work waiting for you!" I could not say anything more to them, but I said to myself, *Yes, we must get to work. There is much work to do where I am going!*

As I departed, with powerful emotions overtaking me, I heard over my shoulder the precious words they all began to sing:

How sweet are the tidings that greet the pilgrim's ear,
As he wanders in exile from home!
Soon, soon will the Savior in glory appear,
And soon will the kingdom come.

He's coming, coming, coming soon I know,
Coming back to this earth again;
And the weary pilgrims will to glory go,
When the Savior comes to reign.[1]

Heading out through the bars of the main gate of the Lion's den, they sang on: "He's coming, coming, coming soon I know." And I shouted back to them with all my strength, "Yes, He's coming! Never lose hope!"

---

1. "How Sweet Are the Tidings," in *The Seventh-day Adventist Hymnal.*

Chapter 13

On Dangerous Ground

Keep me, O LORD, from the hands of the wicked;
preserve me from violent men, who have purposed to make my steps stumble.
The proud have hidden a snare for me, and cords. . . .
I said to the LORD: "You are my God."

—Psalm 140:4–6

The process of transferring to the prison farm where political prisoners did forced labor lasted several hours. The words of Sergeant G. echoed in my mind: *"Son, I have good news and bad news for you."* I began to feel uneasy. *"Now you need to know that when they move you out among the political prisoners, you will be all the more in the crosshairs because there are certain ones planted there who aren't really what they appear to be. They are undercover agents who are responsible for closely monitoring any activity, and they are very skilled; none of us—not even I—know who they are. . . . You are to be considered a counterrevolutionist. . . . They would like to see you get at least twenty years."*

By that time, I knew that the ground I was about to tread was going to be dangerous, and that bothered me somewhat, for it is entirely human to feel certain fears and uncertainties; yet my faith was greatly bolstered, and I had learned well the rules of engagement with challenges in the prison setting. Consequently, my main question was, what is God planning to do next? How is He going to guide me and free me from this absurd and evil trap? They placed me there intentionally to involve me, if possible, with supposedly secret members of the White Rose organization, which was proscribed for being openly opposed to the Castro government. The truth is, I had never even heard of it before then. There were also other prisoners serving sentences for various activities deemed counterrevolutionary; of this I will have more to say later.

Modern Pharisees

The environment was a total minefield, shockingly so. It would be easy for the prison authorities to link me with these political opponents. The fact is that the political prisoners were excellent men of good principles; they were not at all criminals in the normal sense but were incarcerated for their ideological convictions. I really had not even the slightest idea of their situation; I was then, as now, a minister and considered myself apolitical, not wasting my energy fighting either in favor of or against an earthly government. My mission was different and purely spiritual—building the kingdom of God! But this obviously was also considered a crime under the so-called revolutionary government.

Their strategy

Their strategy was to entangle me, if possible, so that new charges could be brought against me for scheming against the revolution. My only option was to fulfill my ministry among the prisoners without giving an opening to my enemies and allowing them to misrepresent my motives or my actions. But who could I trust? The future was uncertain and a little unsettling. I did not know who my enemies might be; I just knew that they were out there, lurking in the shadows, disguised as political prisoners, with hypocritical smiles and treacherous tongues.

Like the Pharisees of old who tried to ensnare Jesus and deliver Him into the clutches of the Sanhedrin, these cunning individuals would make their move against me and try to cause me to fall into their net as part of their design against a servant of the Lord.

In the barracks

Absorbed in these reflections, I was conducted by the guards to the prison farm's barracks. When we entered the area, I heard a booming voice, which suddenly jolted me out of my thoughts. "Pastor Cortés! Pastor Cortés! Is it really you, or am I seeing a vision?"

My first reaction was, *Already my problems begin! Here comes the first trap. If one of these counterrevolutionary prisoners knows me, then I'm in trouble! This gives the prison administrators justification for saying I am one of these fellows. But who could possibly know me here?*

Very soon my doubts would be clarified. The guards left me at the door of one of the barracks and told me this was where I would be staying. "Private Ross will put you to work." They turned and headed back to the prison buildings.

Chapter 14

Mysterious Providences

*"You are my refuge, my portion in the land of the living. Attend to my cry,
for I am brought very low; deliver me from my persecutors, for they are stronger
than I. Bring my soul out of prison, that I may praise Your name;
the righteous shall surround me, for You shall deal bountifully with me."*
—Psalm 142:5–7

In life, sometimes things happen that may seem accidental or coincidental at first glance; but when we analyze these things intelligently with spiritual minds, we come to realize that they are divine providences, and we are awed at how God, who knows the end from the beginning, acts without leaving us to the forces of blind fate. He works out ways to help His children when hard times come, and He provides channels of aid in the face of need.

God opens the way

Let me share a story of divine providence with you from my own experience: It was a summer morning, two years before the events related to my arrest. My wife and I were practically newlyweds. One day we needed to go to a place called Puerto Esperanza on the northwest coast of the province of Pinar del Río. At that time, and I think it is still the same, transportation was very difficult. The bus station in the city of Pinar del Río was crowded with passengers trying to board those rare and rickety Czechoslovakia-manufactured buses, which due to their shape and green paint are called cucumbers. We got up early and headed to the bus station, and after waiting in a long line, we finally got tickets for two seats on a bus heading to our destination. The chugging bus was already crowded with passengers, so the driver didn't stop to pick up any more along the way. But near the provincial hospital, at the junction of the road going to Viñales, two soldiers stopped the bus and climbed aboard with much difficulty. They crammed in two prisoners handcuffed together as well. The prisoners, wearing the typical prison uniforms, looked very haggard and exhausted. Every lurch and turn practically toppled the poor fellows. It was painful to watch their efforts to remain standing, so Celita and I looked at each other and decided to give up our seats for them. That was more an act of compassion than of courtesy. With embarrassment and gratitude, they accepted our seats, and for a brief moment, we struck up a conversation with them. They told us that they had been granted special passes to attend the funeral of their mother, but because the head of the prison didn't care to provide any transportation, they were sent under guard via public transport. This was another way to humiliate and belittle political prisoners. Why bother to send despicable enemies of the revolution by government Jeep even if they were grieving for someone so dear to them as their mother? I told them that we were Pastor and Mrs. José Cortés, from the church located on the highway to Viñales, which we would soon pass and that I was going with my wife to Puerto Esperanza. We promised to pray for them and their family, and they told us their names, Julian and Roman. Then one of the guards, in a very ugly tone, told me that it was forbidden to talk to the prisoners. After that, we exchanged no further words until the day I heard that loud voice.

That loud voice

That's right! The booming voice that called out to me at the entrance to the barracks was the voice of Roman, the younger and heavier of the two imprisoned brothers. "What a small world!" we said in unison. "Or rather, what a big prison," corrected Julian. And we laughed like children, rather than crying at our situation. But of all the strange things that happen in life, this was one of the most fortunate for us all. God's plan for them and for me was taking shape.

I would have the information needed to protect myself from potential enemies, and they would have the spiritual support and the knowledge of the plan of salvation that I could offer them. Both brothers were of great help to me during this difficult stage of my experience among the political prisoners, and more than that, they were the key to opening the way into this incredible and secretive world, where in order to survive one had to distrust everyone inside and outside the circle. Each man had a story, and every story had a plot that was sometimes astonishing and always painful.

That afternoon, after storing my few belongings under the rough plank bunk bed, I spent the day talking with these two brothers who were the only people I already knew. We became real friends and are to this day; I should add that friendship among those political prisoners does not end when one is released or because of the passing of time, no matter how long. We became brothers forever. They gradually introduced me to the rest of the barrack's tenants, whom I got to know by recognizing which ones were or were not reliable. All the inmates showed interest in getting to know the pastor who had arrived, and they especially wanted to know "where I had let the bombs fall"—their way of asking how I, a religious person, managed to end up in a place like this. All without exception were respectful and friendly. It was indeed a very different place compared to section 4.

The manager of the American farm

As you can imagine, the conversation with my two new friends (or old friends, I hardly know what to call them) picked up where we had left off when the guard tongue-lashed us that day in the "cucumber" on our trip to Puerto Esperanza.

The two brothers, Julian and Roman, had been tried and sentenced in a shared trial, each to forty-five years imprisonment for activities against the revolution and national security. They were accused of collusion with an American citizen, the owner of a large tract of land in an area known as Consolación del Norte, near the mountains where insurgents operated. In those days, there were armed groups conducting guerrilla warfare with the intention of overthrowing the revolutionary government.

This is the story told to me by Julian and seconded by his younger brother with a sad tone but far from resignation.

"Yes, I was the general manager of the American farm, or as it was commonly called 'the American's farm,' and my brother Roman was the chief foreman of livestock. This farm was a real pot of gold; it had the best livestock in the western region and probably in the whole island. The dairy and agricultural products for export and for local consumption were truly enviable. All our employees lived well—I am not saying they were rich, but they had everything they needed—and without exception all had decent housing.

"I was a happy man! My wife, whom I adore, and I have three sons who are my pride. We had a big house, painted white, with a tiled roof and sliding doors. The garden was filled with red roses, poppies, and gardenias. We had fruit trees, and in my pasture, there were several fine riding horses. Oh, and my Jeep, what a gem of a vehicle it was! Although it wasn't the latest model, it ran beautifully. All the employees respected and thought highly of me. Mr. Johnson, my employer and the owner of the property, paid me a very decent salary. He trusted me and considered me more like a member of his own family than merely an employee. Everything was so perfect! But then, on that October afternoon, everything began to crumble and disappear as if carried away by a cyclone.

"Three Soviet-made trucks, full of soldiers with rifles, came rolling in. They had in their hands a list of supposed culprits to be arrested, the first being Mr. Johnson. I was the second, then my brother Roman, followed by seven more employees—ten in all. They made us lie facedown on the ground by the front gate. With much violence, they tied our hands behind our backs, one by one. Mrs. Johnson and her household helpers were ordered into a room with several guards until they had finished a search of the premises. When they loaded us onto the trucks to take us away, we noticed on the back of one of the trucks four large crates full of guns, boxes of ammunition, hand grenades, and other such munitions of war. There were files of papers from the administration offices and from my office, along with several thousand dollars in cash. The enraged officer in charge was screaming like crazy and barking out orders. Then with an air of a mission accomplished, he haughtily addressed us: 'At last, we've caught you! Here is the evidence of betrayal that you vile worms have been committing against the honest, hardworking people of Cuba.' Then we realized the enormity of the problem we faced.

"They alleged that Mr. Johnson and his trusted employees had been feeding and arming insurgents in the mountains and that their operation had rounded up plenty of evidence to prove the charges. I can say truthfully that I had never seen any of those arms before. None of the employees, not even Mr. Johnson himself, knew of their existence. My employer was a noble and peaceful man who didn't even own a rifle for hunting. He always said, 'I want no enemies; I need no weapons!' And that was true.

"The Johnsons settled in the northern area of the westernmost province of Cuba in 1949. Thousands of American families did the same after the Second World War, and they began investing their resources in the then-prosperous island. It is conveniently close to the United States, only ninety miles away, and with very low costs to and from the continent. In those days, you could fly from Havana to Key West for just ten dollars, yes, only ten dollars! Many times we flew to Florida to buy equipment or materials and returned home the same day," Julian reminisced with eyes full of longing. "The influence of this family had been of benefit to many in the region. But now this unexpected enemy appeared. Land expropriations and interventions were carried out by the INRA [the initials in Spanish for the National Institute of Agrarian Reform]. But due to certain high-level negotiations with the government, they had never touched the American farm. But now all that was at an end; before any further strategies for defense could be organized, the Communist authorities made this decisive strike.

"I am convinced that this was all a fabrication; Mr. Johnson would have made me aware of any political activity or support for the rebels if he had been involved. He was a responsible, respectful, and sensitive person. Moreover, on that farm, nothing entered or went out that I would not have seen. No cattle ever went missing or were slaughtered to feed any guerrillas, as was claimed. No shipment of arms had ever entered the farm. And additionally, how could we have obtained Soviet-made weapons such as those? Only the army had them! No money had been allocated for any such activity. It was all a farce. But truthfulness meant nothing to the almost illiterate official spewing forth his pronouncements as if he were a judge: 'This degenerate gringo is on the side of Yankee imperialism. It's going to go very bad for him. Although we know that he is from there, and he is theirs. But you are from here; you are traitors! You are unpatriotic scum! It's going to go even worse for you; you'll rot behind bars.'

"And now, as you can see, that is exactly what is happening. Here we are, prisoners taken away from our families, with no hope of release and at the mercy of a government that hates us for no reason. We've been here fifteen years, and we have thirty more to go on our forty-five-year sentence, if God grants us life. I was thirty-five and my brother Roman was thirty-two when we fell into this misfortune. It's better not to think about that or do the math, because it's highly likely that the only way we are leaving here is in a coffin to the cemetery! It would be very difficult in these conditions to survive to eighty; and even if we could, what would we be good for then?"

My friends were strong men inured by the hardships of prison; they did not cry. Instead, they just clenched their jaws and sighed deeply, like the snort of a warhorse facing the rigors of battle. That was their reality—brutal, atrocious, unpalatable, but unavoidable.

I listened for a long time as they told their stories one after another, sometimes causing me anguish and sometimes filling me with admiration. They spoke as if in a set pattern—taking turns as one would speak, while the other caught his breath, never contradicting each other. Sometimes they spoke as a duo. Really it gave me chills to see and hear men in their condition saying such things as they had shared with me. Their manly honesty won my empathy, and it seems to me that God looked down at me from heaven and winked, saying, "There, you now have these! Help them!"

Again I could see God's plan very clearly and the reason behind my time in that unjust place. They needed *something* in order to continue their difficult existence, and that *something*, which is so important in the life of every person, certainly was essential for Julian, for Roman, and for many others I was soon to become acquainted with in that place. It was nothing less than the good news of salvation. I do not mean to imply that those men were unbelievers—not at all. Julian had said, "I know that something has to exist," and Roman had added, "I believe in God in my own way, although He has forgotten me."

When it was finally my turn to speak, I began at a measured pace: "Friends, I want to bestow on you a gift; but as I have nothing material to offer and there is no human power that can solve our current situation, I'm going to give you a piece of wisdom that I am sure you will appreciate a great deal. Listen because this is the Word of God." I repeated from memory these passages that helped me in my darkest moments and which I still keep in my heart, because they speak of my hope—the hope that never disappoints even in the most fearful situations:

"I cry out to the LORD with my voice;
With my voice to the LORD I make my supplication.
I pour out my complaint before Him;
I declare before Him my trouble.

"When my spirit was overwhelmed within me,
Then You knew my path.
In the way in which I walk
They have secretly set a snare for me.
Look on my right hand and see,
For there is no one who acknowledges me;
Refuge has failed me;
No one cares for my soul.

"I cried out to You, O LORD:
I said, 'You are my refuge,
My portion in the land of the living.
Attend to my cry,
For I am brought very low;
Deliver me from my persecutors,
For they are stronger than I.
Bring my soul out of prison,
That I may praise Your name;
The righteous shall surround me,
For You shall deal bountifully with me' " (Psalm 142:1–7).

These words were written by the psalmist David when he was hiding in a cave while being unjustly persecuted by King Saul and at a time when he was in mortal distress. Now they came as refreshing water to the thirsty souls of my fellow sufferers. A miracle began to happen from that encounter with the Word of God. God visited them, and gradually they were transformed and became two men of faith who thereafter began to minister to the other inmates. They also encountered a new reason to live, and after being baptized secretly in a stream's pool on the way to the quarry, their testimony was truly impressive. They spoke with extraordinary power, as "rivers of living water" started flowing from within them (John 7:38). For in them, it came to pass what Jesus said: " 'If anyone thirsts, let him come to Me and drink. He who believes in Me, as the Scripture has said, out of his heart will flow rivers of living water.' But this He spoke concerning the Spirit, whom those believing in Him would receive" (John 7:37–39).

Because of this and many other things, I believe in conversion to God and in the transformation that comes by accepting Jesus Christ as Savior and Lord. I have seen and I have lived this. It is wonderful to behold and experience the touch of the Divine Hand, which is able to lift a human being from the bottom of the cruelest abyss, release that person from sadness and despair, and set him or her on a path full of light, hope, and victory.

There are moments in the lives of humans, and there are moments in the lives of nations, when all seems lost—we can find no recourse; there is no one to whom we can appeal; we are wrapped in darkness; and uncertainty oppresses the heart. This is especially so when those moments turn into days, stretching on into weeks, months, and seemingly unending years, and then on the horizon, even larger numbers of years accumulate, surpassing what has already transpired, with no hint of the possibility of reprieve. Then the pain and resentment become unbearable; the anguish is indescribable; and the situation becomes mentally untenable. But, for such horrible realities as these, God created hope. It is real, and we must hold on to this glorious expectation as the only sure anchor for the soul. Whether we are guilty or not, it does not matter; the wonderful grace of God intervenes in our behalf. That ineffable gift is available to the innocent, yes, but it obstinately seeks out the guilty as well and offers even these His gracious solution. Many people do not understand this because they perceive the Lord to be an implacable judge, One who is looking for any excuse to condemn us. That's what the devil wants us to believe because it allows him to heap all the more mental suffering on us. This leads to depression, even suicide, and finally eternal loss. But learn this wonderful truth, my dear friend: God loves the sinner, and He goes in search of the guilty, the rebellious, the convicted offender, as well as the political prisoner, for in Jesus Christ there is hope for them all! No matter how long or oppressive the condemnation, no prison irons in the entire world can chain down the hope-filled soul's Godward thoughts! In Christ, there is freedom! I later learned that many of those who were sentenced to death, when they were tied to the stake before the firing squad, filled with faith shouted out at the crack of the rifles: "King Jesus Lives!"

Chapter 15

Hard Work

"Come to Me, all you who labor and are heavy laden, and I will give you rest. Take My yoke upon you and learn from Me, for I am gentle and lowly in heart, and you will find rest for your souls. For My yoke is easy and My burden is light."
—Matthew 11:28–30

T he next morning, while it was still quite dark, the siren sounded, indicating it was time to get up. We had only fifteen minutes to wash, get dressed, and line up for our frugal breakfast, which consisted of a piece of bread with the faintest touch of butter and a jug of milk with a bland flavor; however, it was certainly more abundant than inside the prison. The regulations indicated fifteen minutes for breakfast and then we had to report to work, but it never took that long to eat the meal. Soon Lieutenant Manuel appeared and gave me orders to report to Private Ross to work with his squad. "We'll see if you can handle it out here. This isn't work for sissy pastors. This is men's work! Be warned because I'm going to 'checkmate' you, Pastor!"

Pick, shovel, sledgehammer, and steel bar

Private Ross's brigade was assigned to build a new access road to the farm. The old road had deteriorated greatly during the rainy season; it needed to be maintained and kept in good condition so that trucks could get through to the poultry section. This work would not have been difficult under normal conditions; but under the pretext that the administration did not have the resources to bring in the appropriate equipment, it had to be done using the most rudimentary means imaginable. None of the prisoners believed that line; everyone knew it was pure punishment. To prepare the roadbed without a grader or tractor, we had to use our own hands and backs, working with picks and shovels. For hauling dirt from high spots to low areas, they provided some crude wheelbarrows with iron wheels, which were always getting mired in the mud. It would take several of us to push and pull those contraptions while Private Ross constantly shouted and the guards mocked us. It was very tiring work. When we had a section of the roadway ready to be surfaced, variable sized rock was brought in from the quarry on a wagon pulled by oxen. We had sledgehammers and steel bars to work the rough material into shape for a tolerably acceptable surface. On that first day, I found the early morning hours with the fresh air and the sunlight invigorating. But as midday and afternoon wore on, it was grueling under the scorching sun, especially with no hat or gloves for protection. My unaccustomed hands began to hurt and blister from the sharp edges of the rocks and the friction of the pick and shovel handles. My back ached tremendously that night.

The next day I tied some rags around my bloody hands and headed out to the site. Lieutenant Manuel had it right, this was "men's work" for sure; but he should have called it "slave labor." I gave it my best, nevertheless, and made no complaints like some of the others. Philippians 4:13 kept running through my mind: "I can do all things through Christ who strengthens me." I also recalled the famous phrase from José Martí: "Griping brings dishonor, for that reason I make no complaint." I was determined to hold my own among the workers, and that was my constant prayer to the Lord; I didn't want to dishonor Him in front of the men or the guards. I'd never done that kind of work before, and though it was brutal at first, after a while I hardened up. My strength and energy developed rapidly despite all the previous time in confinement in section 4. It wasn't long until my hands were as calloused as anyone's and they no longer bothered me.

This "sissy pastor," as Lieutenant Manuel scorned me, was determined to prove that in addition to preaching and teaching I could also do many other things. For example, one day the cart got stuck, and the oxen's yoke broke because of all the pulling. With his usual gruffness, Private Ross demanded, "Do any of you men know how to make a yoke?" But no one knew how. Finally, I spoke up: "I've never done that, but if you give me a helper and some tools we should be able to make one. We'll need a good piece of wood, a pencil, a saw, some chisels, and a hand plane to do the job." All I said was done. The next morning we had a makeshift carpentry shop set up under some *atejes* trees, which are typical to that area, and Julian and I got down to work. We went to great pains to make that yoke as perfect as possible; and not to brag, but it seemed to me that ours was a much better one than the original model we worked from. It looked like a piece of art. The first one was made of oak, later we made another from mahogany. The yokes were so good and classy that they drew the admiration of all, including the reeducator who admitted behind my back that "this pastor is solid."

Somewhat amazed or annoyed, Julian questioned me at times, "Teacher, why do you go to such efforts to do things so well for people who are so bad?"

My response was biblical: "Julian, I do not want to work just for man's approval but for God's honor."

"How so?" my friend wondered.

"The Bible teaches us that whatever we do, we should do it to the best of our ability, which means we must do our work not just to please people but that we should always remember we are serving Christ and working from the heart according to the will of God [Ephesians 6:6]. And if something is worth doing, it is worth doing well. I'm not doing this so much for them as I am doing it for myself and for God. He should be glorified in all our actions."

Private Ross

Something bothered me about Private Ross's attitude. All the men resented him; nobody understood him; and yet everyone respected him. He was also a political prisoner. No one doubted his integrity, but he worked like a man possessed. He always had a sad and bitter countenance, and nobody had seen him smile in years. He was capable of any sacrifice, ready to put his own life on the line, as they say, to save a companion; yet he was also the cruel boss of the entire farm brigade, the equivalent of the galley chief inside the prison. He forced his men to work like animals. He was serving a life sentence, but he never spoke to anyone about the reason behind that or about his private life. All that we knew was that he had been a captain under the command of General Tabernilla of the Joint General Staff, during the rule of Fulgencio Batista y Zaldivar. The mock rank of "Private" Ross was imposed on him during his imprisonment on Isla de Pinos, the first place where he was taken after his conviction. The prison guards commented that having been a captain, a career soldier, he was degraded and condemned for betraying his country and in derision he would be called "Private" for the rest of his life. In that way, they deliberately humiliated this man and sought to destroy the self-esteem of one who had dedicated his life to a military career. Now the only command he was given was this brigade of fellow prisoners.

Other than formalities and brief instructions on the day I was entrusted with the job of making the yokes for the oxcart, there was no further opportunity to exchange any words with him.

God provides an opportunity

There came a rainy morning when all the prisoners had to stay in the barracks; some rested, and others spent the time in conversations. I decided to go out to the makeshift carpentry shop and polish up the ox yoke. There I found Private Ross. That was when God gave me the opportunity to speak to him; I'm convinced it was no mere coincidence. Realizing that there might not be another chance as ideal as that, I chose my words carefully, hoping to break through his protective shell. Having heard some commentaries about him, I suspected that there could possibly be a link between him and a certain relative of mine.

"You know, Mr. Ross," I said quite directly, "I have an uncle who was for many years the staff secretary to General Tabernilla there in Colombia.* Maybe you got to know him." In that precise moment, a bolt of lightning flashed across the sky, followed by a tremendous clap of thunder. It seemed to shake him out of his preoccupation. "Who are you talking about? Sergeant Major José Angel Sosa?"

"Exactly," I replied. "Sergeant Major José Angel Sosa."

"He was my good friend, but I never heard from him again after the Bay of Pigs. What a decisive and courageous fellow he was. I regret that I did not share his vision and follow his advice. If I had, I probably would not find myself here!"

His words then poured out, rough as usual, like one who doesn't want to speak but has to get it out. He swore, spit on the ground, and shuffled his boot upon the dirt, letting out his pent-up emotion, I suppose. That moment is still vivid in my memory. He took a pause and then replied with heavy, melancholy words: "I could have been with them!" He paused again, and then he poured forth a flood of questions in a very personal tone: "How is the sergeant major? Where does he live? What happened to Carmen and the children? He has two beautiful daughters and a son who is his great pride. But could they finally leave and go to be with him? Please tell me about them!"

"My captain," I said, "have patience, and I will tell you everything I know about my uncle Angel" (as my sisters and I called him).

"According to the latest letters that my mother and grandmother have received, they are fine and are now living in a city called Rochester in upstate New York in the United States. He works for the General Motors Corporation."

"The sergeant major was smarter than me," he said in his gruff voice, which was mellowing slightly with a touch of cordial civility. "He didn't trust any of them; he didn't trust the presumed justice of the new revolutionary government, much less the promises of personal security given by Camilo Cienfuegos, who was the best of the commanders of the revolution. Sergeant Major Sosa came to visit me at my house one afternoon—I still lived in Colombia, Las Tunas. He warned me that we had only a short window of time to get out of the country. He urged me to leave as the witch hunt was about to start. 'If we don't get out now, there will be nothing we can do to regain the freedom of Cuba. Martyrs serve to inspire the people, but live soldiers will be needed. Leave now, or you won't ever be able to. It is the only option; we will need to organize and then come back in strength!' That was the last time I saw him. Later I learned that the sergeant major had gone to the United States. He could foresee what I could not; he could see the danger."

---

* This Colombia is a municipality in the Cuban province of Las Tunas, about six miles (ten kilometers) south of Guáimaro.

Career soldiers

"We two, like many others, were professional soldiers; neither the politicians in turn or the corrupt ones at the top were pleased about our rank or our positions. We were from the military academy, and the nature of our work was mainly administrative. We were never engaged in combat with the revolutionary army, and above all, there was no blood on our hands and no theft. We were always men of integrity, impeccable in our military calling. For this reason, Camilo Cienfuegos offered us the possibility to remain in service, and I decided to stay, along with my family. We lived well; my wife was accustomed to every luxury and was not willing to go to the United States to start over from scratch. She did not want to be an immigrant in a country where a different language was spoken. I was weak in the face of her insistence and decided that we would wait quietly and trust that everything would work out. I definitely was not a politician but a military man; I personally disliked the previous dictator, Fulgencio Batista, and considered it a disgrace that he occupied the Presidential Palace. I sincerely hoped that the words of the new commander in chief, who came offering a better life and bearing in his soul the doctrines of the master, would produce prosperity and peace, which I had always desired for my people. But that did not last long, and in a few months, I realized my big mistake.

"My presence 'was not wanted' in the new General Staff. The nonsense of the new leaders—some of them were only semiliterate—was amazing; their haughty attitudes of self-reliance mixed with ignorance led them to make catastrophic decisions. The direction they were taking was leading toward total chaos; but they were drunk with power, and nothing could make them think right. The few times I tried to offer an opinion, my ideas were described as tainted with the old ways. The few carryover officials still in service were stigmatized as a necessary evil to facilitate the transfer of power. We had barely survived the first wave of 'purification' of the army. Very few were simply relieved of their responsibilities and allowed to go into civilian life; the vast majority were prosecuted and imprisoned for real or imaginary reasons. Of the nearly one thousand who were prosecuted, more than half have been killed, and many of them simply by decree. And to this day, I do not know who the lucky ones are, the dead or those who have to live on in this wretched life."

The firing squad

"Five of my subordinates were taken to the execution wall at La Cabaña because of my lack of vision. I urged them not to leave, that I needed them to stay in service, that Cuba needed them, and they stayed with me until it was too late. It was all so unfair; they were good men, fine family men, and now they are dead. Do you understand what I'm saying? They are dead, and I'm still here—the living dead. But I continue to hear them calling out to me from their graves.

In all these years, I have not had peace of mind. I can never look into the eyes of those widows and those orphans! Never!" As he spoke those words, two tears streaked down his weathered face. Then ashamed of himself and like a defeated warrior, he turned and sought to escape my presence.

Captain Ross

I do not want to think where this man might have ended up, with his load of anguish and grief, if I had not stopped him. With an imperious tone, I exclaimed, "Captain Ross, do not leave! I have a message from General Jesus for you." He turned on his heel, as in the old days, and said, "If that is so, I will listen; but do not call me 'Captain,' I do not deserve it." Then God gave me the words this troubled man needed to hear: "Come to Me, all you who labor and are heavy laden, and I will give you rest. Take My yoke upon you and learn from Me, for I am gentle and lowly in heart, and you will find rest for your souls. For My yoke is easy and My burden is light" (Matthew 11:28–30).

"I can see that your burdens are many; you need to accept the offer of Christ: 'Take My yoke,' " and then I pointed to the yoke I was polishing. "Look, the yoke has two oxbows, but you are trying to carry this burden alone. Jesus offers to put His neck in the other oxbow and pull together with you. That will greatly lighten your burden, for His yoke makes it much easier for you."

The man sat down and said, "You are a total stranger; but something tells me that I should listen to you. I suppose I have nothing to lose."

"Mr. Ross, we all have much to lose but also much to gain in this war, which is a spiritual war above all. We have to win our souls for the kingdom of heaven. This struggle is not against flesh and blood; it is against the powers of darkness [Ephesians 6:12]. This is much bigger than what we've been talking about and goes far beyond what anyone could imagine. The reality of what I want to present to you is far greater than the problems we have in Cuba or in any other country, and it is vastly more serious than any political dilemma we face. All this is temporary and transient. We see the faces of people that hurt us today, including Castro and his followers, but those detestable people are nothing in themselves, rather they are victims of spiritual wickedness. Many of them would be horrified if they could see the overall plot, the war they are in, and who is the one actually controlling them. Of course, they are responsible for allowing themselves to be manipulated.

"The Bible speaks of a cosmic conflict that is taking place in the universe. It is the great age-old struggle between good and evil, and what is at stake is of eternal significance. A wrongful conviction? A life sentence? A firing squad? True, all of this is horrible! There is no justification for it! But no matter how monstrous and inhuman it appears to us, it still pales in comparison with eternity and the destiny of all humanity! Yes, Mr. Ross, this issue goes far beyond what we can see with our human eyes."

"And what about those who were killed, and those who are dying?" he broke in. "Those are left without compensation, because death has no solution!"

"The only death that has no solution," I said, "is eternal death. But death as we know it presently is nothing more than a conquered foe; it is just like a dream that we wake up from on the day of resurrection because Jesus Christ overcame death by His own death on the cross of Calvary. Listen, this is the Word of God! The hope of the resurrection is the antidote for death in all its shapes and forms.

"Behold, I tell you a mystery: We shall not all sleep, but we shall all be changed—in a moment, in the twinkling of an eye, at the last trumpet. For the trumpet will sound, and the dead will be raised incorruptible, and we shall be changed. For this corruptible must put on incorruption, and this mortal must put on immortality. So when this corruptible has put on incorruption, and this mortal has put on immortality, then shall be brought to pass the saying that is written: 'Death is swallowed up in victory.'

'O Death, where is your sting?
O Hades, where is your victory?'

"The sting of death is sin, and the strength of sin is the law. But thanks be to God, who gives us the victory through our Lord Jesus Christ" (1 Corinthians 15:51–57).

The perspective God offers

"Our existence is not as simple and materialistic as some would have us believe; do not think for a moment that we are merely worthless subjects—perhaps like insects hit by a truck, and then nothing more. We are expensive and valuable beings created in the image of God, who loves us as His children. He knows our names and where we live, and He is fully aware of our anguish and tears. The blood of the martyrs was not shed in vain. Abusers and criminals of every period of history will face the penetrating glare of a just God. Not a single sparrow falls to the ground without it being noticed by the Creator [see Matthew 10:29]. All our sufferings and our tears are captured in a vial by the Lord [see Psalm 56:8]. We are an important part of God's grand plan, despite all the problems we face as a direct result of sin. God's plan will be fulfilled for all of His creation. Understand this: today God opens a new perspective for you! God wants to forgive you, but you must forgive yourself as well. Wallowing in self-pity leads to emotional defeat; live no longer regretting a past for which there is nothing you can do. The present and the future need us. Here are all these people who need hope to go on living, faith to face their difficulties, and trust in God to triumph. You are in charge of them, but you have nothing to offer, and you are suffering because of that. The only cure that exists to overcome and eradicate Communism and all its evil consequences for eternity is the hope that keeps us steady in the midst of the storm, because that is the anchor for the soul. Hope is always accompanied by love and faith in the Creator. These three virtues combined strengthen the weak human being, even if he is a prisoner or suffering from some sickness, and transform him into an invincible warrior of truth, against which executioners are impotent. When we are able to believe, we breathe the scent of eternity in our existence.

"I firmly believe that God has a plan of action for you. I do not think it was just chance that we find ourselves talking about such important matters under these trees. Today God is calling you to be His servant. He wants you to become a spiritual leader for this group of men." I'm not sure how long we spoke as the rain fell, but it was for more than an hour. Then I stood up, and without knowing why, the Spirit came over me in an amazing way, making me speak in terms like these: "As a minister of the gospel and in the name of the General of heaven, I invest you with your rank of captain once again today to care for and serve these people with compassion and to help them direct their lives according to the gospel of the Lord Jesus Christ." Then I asked him to stand up. I put my hand on his shoulder and prayed for him, with a fervor that could shake the very stones under our feet. At the end, I confirmed him: "My brother, Captain Ross, I give you a hug of commission! God sent me here as a pastor to do a strange and special work, and you are an essential element of God's plan."

The man was deeply moved and babbled excitedly: "Teacher, I do not know what I'm feeling here in my chest, something new and wonderful. But even if I believe in God, I know nothing of religion or the gospel. How can I accept this assignment?"

Then I assured him with the promise to teach him the gospel message. "Just let the love of God manifest itself in your life and in your dealings with all these men. Are you willing, Captain Ross?"

"Yes, I agree," he said, saluting in his best military style!

Unusual solutions

Julian, who had been watching from a distance, came and joined us at that moment. We shared with him the highlights of our conversation, and then he also gave the captain a fraternal hug of acceptance. I know that the church does not grant military ranks, but for unconventional circumstances God provides unusual solutions.

A persistent drizzle continued falling while we entered the barracks where almost all our fellow sufferers were present. Julian suddenly and unexpectedly took the initiative and said, "Everyone, please listen up! I have orders from above to inform you that from today forward we are not to address our boss as 'Private'; that term is completely forbidden. From now on, he will be called by the rightful rank that belongs to him: 'Captain Ross.' " And grinning, he uttered an oath against anyone who might fail to obey the order, but it is best we not publish his exact words in this book, even though we are telling the stories of convicts. The group applauded cheerfully, and the captain humbly ambled over to his resting place. From that day on, we all respectfully addressed him as Captain Ross.

Captain Ross's spiritual growth took its time, but it was constant from that day. Daily Bible studies were held beneath those *atejes* trees, and the change was so noticeable that all the inmates were greatly impressed and the name of God was glorified. The man learned to smile, and before long, he was secretly baptized in a stream's pool on the way to the quarry. He began to testify about the name of Jesus and His mercy, "which became manifest in a miserable sinner like me," as he unabashedly proclaimed. Captain Ross always spoke bluntly with conviction and without fear. When Julian advised him to act prudently to avoid problems with the authorities, he responded, "I have nothing to lose—my sentence is for life anyway—but I have a lot to gain: many prisoners for the kingdom of heaven! There we will have eternal freedom. And if I was baptized in secret, it was only to protect the teacher, not because I am afraid or ashamed of what I am now!"

Let me offer a word of hope to those who think it is impossible to change, for those who feel life seems to show no mercy and are resentful, sad, and in conflict within themselves, with humanity, or even with God Himself: If the hardened and bitter former "Private" Ross could not only change his gruffness but experience a marked transformation inwardly and outwardly, then anyone can be transformed by God's love and mercy! It's all about opening the heart ever so slightly to let a ray of light slip in, and God will do the rest. Today I invite you to give it a try; wonderful things will then happen in you!

Chapter 16

And Forgive Us Our Debts

"Our Father in heaven, hallowed be Your name. Your kingdom come.
Your will be done on earth as it is in heaven. Give us this day our daily bread.
And forgive us our debts, as we forgive our debtors."
—Matthew 6:9–12

All these events did not pass by totally unnoticed by the reeducator or by the political commissar, but somehow God was still achieving His purposes despite these most dangerous adversaries. One afternoon these two came to meet with the prisoners and propose a plan to them. With much enthusiasm, they announced a chess championship. At that time, several Russian masters of chess had appeared on the Cuban cultural-political scene. They called it the "scientific game," and all the Cuban political leaders suddenly became fans of the sport, just as they did with any craze coming out of the failed socialist bloc. Fanaticism—whether political or religious or of any other sort—is dangerous and can lead people, who under normal circumstances might be quite decent, to commit the gravest errors and even atrocious crimes.

When these two came announcing their intention to entertain while also educating the prisoners, we instinctively knew that something bad was lurking behind the apparently positive objective they were pushing.

After learning that the reeducator himself would participate in the event, several men signed on, in part to learn and participate but most of all with the secret intention of beating their oppressors at the game. What especially prompted the prisoners to join the competition was that the reeducator boasted it would demonstrate the superior mental skills of the revolutionary intellect compared to the decadent inferiority of the "old scourge." He and his colleagues would represent the new, improved class, while we, naturally, would represent the defeated enemies of the revolution.

Even though I had learned to play the game as a child, I decided to stay out of the controversy because I always had reservations about it being too time consuming, and I preferred to use any leisure time for spiritual pursuits and reading. But in a few days, my colleagues and I realized that the not-so-subtle strategy of the prison administration was to ensnare us. What they were trying to do, among other things, was to worm their way into the minds of the inmates, provoke a spirit of competition so as to divide the attention of the group, and neutralize the influence of the religious work, which they knew was going on. They hoped to create a situation or obtain leads to help them find some evidence to use against me. The conversion of Captain Ross especially riled them; his change was so amazing that they couldn't help but take note. It exasperated them that the prisoners had started calling him "Captain" when their senior official was merely a lieutenant. This official threatened us with reprisals, but my fellow sufferers refused to yield. For me, it was quite clear he wanted to find reasons to cause problems for me, and it sounded like an open challenge when, looking directly at me, he said, "From now on, I will be spending more time here, and it's going to be 'checkmate,' Pastor." This was consistent with what Sergeant G. had forewarned me about.

Thereafter, they scheduled mandatory afternoon practice sessions for "educational" chess. This made it more difficult to conduct Bible studies because the visits of the commissar were almost daily, and the reeducator wasted more than three hours of our time every afternoon conducting his infamous classes in preparation for the championship of the scientific game. The prisoners began to suspect that the reeducator's intentions were not games but politics, and they paid him little attention. They made fun of Lieutenant Manuel under their breath and some out loud for all of his prattle about castles, knights, and rooks. The absolute majority of my fellow prisoners were intelligent men with a certain degree of culture; they were not ignorant about the game. They had suffered from the many wiles of the enemy. Antonio Mujica, a dark-skinned, gray-haired, and clear-thinking inmate who had suffered the loss of an eye to the butt of a guard's rifle, summed up the present situation perfectly: "Gentlemen, we have lived long within this monster, and I know very well its bowels. This man used to come once or twice a week to do his work, and now he comes every day, trying to eat into our brains. Don't give him the time of day. Let him go toot his horn elsewhere!" So from then on, the men, who played a little chess on their own, put the board and pieces away when they saw the reeducator coming, as if the scientific game was of no interest to them.

The mentality of the political prisoner in Cuba is very special and very strong. It is difficult to understand this mentality from the outside. Someone may betray the prisoner from within the group, but very few can be tricked by the ploys of the administrators. I was deeply impressed by a bold scheme Antonio and Ramon came up with and proposed to me: "Teacher, why don't you represent us all in the tournament against the reeducator? He says he will show who has the superior mental capabilities during the championship. He believes the Marxist man formed by the revolution possesses a stronger intellect than does a man of the defeated so-called old scourge. While we've been pretending to learn the game, he has gone on and on with this political superiority nonsense, and now it seems to us that you are just the man to face off with him as our representative in the tournament. You can beat this big shot who thinks to reeducate us when he is such a half-wit himself."

My answer was clear, and I thought conclusive: "Forget it, Brothers, I am a pastor, not a chess player." However, to be sociable, I sometimes played a game or two with some of them, especially with Andres Peralta who had a special fondness for chess and a great need for friendship and companionship.

Request of a dying man

The request I want to tell you about came from Andres Peralta, the only man I saw literally die in prison. I met him while he was working in the quarry during the time when we were building the access road to the penitentiary farm. He was about thirty-seven years old, white skin, black hair, and quite athletic; he was a hardworking and reserved man. During that time, I never had a chance to engage him in conversation, but later he became my unconditional friend. Julian told me about him: "He is a serious and enigmatic man. He was in solitary confinement for more than four years while waiting for the review of his case, and after the hearing, he was sentenced to twenty years imprisonment. A year ago he was transferred here. We know that he was living in the United States, returned to Cuba on a speedboat, and was captured on the beach at Mariel. He speaks English as well as Spanish; he reminds me a lot of my former employer, the American. He is accused of being trained as an agent of the Central Intelligence Agency, but he has always denied that, saying it's not true and that he only committed the madness of coming over in his boat, to see his mother for the last time as she was dying of cancer in the province of Havana. This he did, he says, because after more than three years of trying to get permission to come to Cuba legally, he was denied. Finally, his mother died, but as he was then being held in solitary confinement, he wasn't permitted to go see her on her deathbed. Andres was deeply affected by the fact that the warden wouldn't grant him special permission even to attend her funeral at the petition of his aunts and other relatives. This has produced in him bitter resentment and hatred."

Andres and I spent many hours talking about spiritual subjects and studying the Bible, but the issue of forgiveness was his stumbling block. "How can I forgive these thugs who think they own the lives of others? God can't have mercy on them, and neither do I."

That was the way things stood until the day it happened. But what was it that happened?

I still remember that fateful afternoon. How could I forget it? For several days the visit of the reviled director had been announced. "Keep everything clean and orderly," the guards told us. "Comrade First Lieutenant, the Director of the prison, will make a special visit, and we are favored to win recognition as the most efficient prison in all of Cuba. And with him are coming men from the National Bureau of Prisons and the Ministry of the Interior."

"What does that matter to us?" groused the prisoners between clenched teeth.

The inmates hated the director and called him by a nickname that naturally bothered me because I personally disapprove of offensive names; but these are the facts, so I'll just tell it like it is. Due to the flat broadness of his nose plus his reputation for cruelty, everyone called him "Shovel Face the Abuser," or simply "Shovel Face." (Even some of the guards who did not like the man called him that but obviously behind his back.) I'm sure the director had overheard the term at times, and it no doubt rankled him.

The prisoners were all ordered to wear clean uniforms and keep the barracks neat. Orders such as those were hardly necessary because in the political section, except on rare exceptions, all the men habitually kept themselves and their surroundings in top form.

That afternoon seemed to be a holiday for our jailers, but it would witness a daring and tragic event. Everyone was to be present in the zinc-roofed wooden galley, which served as the mess hall, to witness the visit of the senior prison authorities.

The big day arrived, and presentations were made, including information about many supposedly positive achievements of the revolution. With respect to the task of reeducating the prison population, opportunities were announced for those who were ready to board the train of the victorious revolutionary proletariat. On that occasion, some of the inmates who were nothing more than infiltrators began offering their testimonies of gratitude to the commander in chief, to the prison management, and to the reeducators who had helped them understand their past mistakes. These were rewarded with transfers to lower security prisons with fewer restrictions, while others would receive sentence reductions. But we prisoners knew that all this was just a comedic performance to extract their imbedded informers because their work among us was finished.

Then came the highlight of the tragicomedy, the act in which one of the visitors began to bestow accolades for the good work, dedication, and fairness of the Director of the prison. It was such a farce, and we found it extremely ridiculous and irritating. All the prisoners were rolling their eyes and biting their tongues, when suddenly, a husky, resonant voice shouted from the back of the room: "Shovel Face! Abuser! Murderer!" All of us were surprised; some were petrified; and many began to laugh heartily and applaud. The officers became angry and frantic. The director, perhaps recognizing that these attributes were real, commanded silence and said, "Whoever said that, if he's a real man, come up here and say it to my face. I am going to reward him with a bag of sugar and a roll of cigars!"

The moment was very tense. I thought no one would speak up, but then we saw with dismay that Andres Peralta stepped forward and got right up in the director's face and shouted three times with marked emphasis, "Shovel Face! Abuser! Murderer! Shovel Face! Abuser! Murderer! Shovel Face! Abuser! Murderer!" I think he would have continued shouting it all afternoon if they did not stop him.

The only response was, "Take him away, and wait for me." The reeducator, with his heavy revolver in his hand, as if fearing a revolt, hit Andres in the face, and several guards subdued the prisoner and led him away.

The great celebration ended in a verbal melee with offenses and insults. The threats of the punishment for the mocking laughter and applause would be fulfilled to the letter—suspension of family visits, harder work, and reduced food rations. But the saddest thing happened about three hours later, almost ten at night, the usual hour to turn the lights off and ring a bell indicating bedtime. Guards carried in the bruised and broken body of Andres on a stretcher. He had bandages on his head, arms, and legs; his face was unrecognizable, and he appeared to be unconscious. Behind his stretcher came a kitchen worker pushing a wheelbarrow with a sack of sugar and a full roll of cigars—how insulting! They hefted Andres onto his bunk and placed beside him those trophies, which he would never sample, and I doubt he would have ever cared to anyway. Andres was too dignified for that. But something interesting happened: none of the other prisoners ever touched that sugar or those cigars either, even though they were considered highly desirable items in prison.

Andres Peralta set free

Julian and I did not leave our companion's side. Andres was terribly battered and bruised; they had literally smashed him to pieces—the bandages covering his head were saturated in blood. No painkiller was provided to ease in the slightest his suffering. The entire group was in shock, and none could even think of trying to sleep. We all feared the worst would happen, and so it was to be. I think that the beating he suffered caused severe damage to his internal organs, and because of the hemorrhaging, he was nearing his end.

"Andres," I said to him, grabbing his hand firmly and compassionately, "are you ready for what's going to happen?" Then weakly and barely breathing, he replied, "Yes, I did pretty much all I could. My original mission failed." For obvious reasons, I didn't want to know what his "original mission" was, and even if I knew that, I would not share it here. Then he began to sob a little before regaining his composure as best he could and exclaimed, "But at least I shouted in his face what he deserved to hear, which no one had ever told him face-to-face before! I knew what would happen to me, but that's for the best. Soon I will leave this prison—I'm no good at being a prisoner—I'm leaving here free! No one can go on holding the dead as prisoners. Now I want to ask two favors: pray for me so that I can rest in peace until the day of resurrection. I need to forgive them, and I want God to forgive me too." The group of brothers surrounded the cot where Andres lay at the verge of departure, but I thanked the Lord because the only impediment had been removed for Brother Andres to meet his God and feel inner peace. He was able to forgive and be forgiven in his last moments! We prayed fervently for our dying companion: "Our Father in heaven. . . . Forgive us our debts, as we forgive our debtors." We talked with God for a long time. I don't know how long it was, but he seemed relieved, his agony was calmed, and he added his amens several times. Then he wanted to speak a few more words; drawing up the last of his strength, he said, "I have now forgiven them; but that other guy who hit me in the face with his revolver, show him what a loser he is. Beat him in the chess championship!"

"But Andres, what's to be gained?"

"Teacher," he said, "that's the only way to tell these people that they are wrong! That although they seized power by force and deception, they are not superior! You promise me this." More to calm his agitation than because I had intentions of doing what he asked, I agreed: "Yeah, OK; I promise." He thanked me, squeezed my hand weakly, and said no more. Minutes later we realized that he had stopped breathing. Andres Peralta had been released.

We alerted the guard in the security tower. Without registering even the slightest hint of compassion, he limited his comments to a cold, perfunctory response: "We already knew that would happen. And it will happen to anyone else who does the same! We'll just leave him there until the morning to teach you a lesson you won't forget."

I must confess that things like that can test the most saintly of persons, and that wouldn't be me. The lack of sensitivity that some supposed human beings are capable of exhibiting when they are armed with weapons and have the force of the government behind them is shameful in the extreme. We had no other recourse, so we decided to remain together in a circle around the dead body of our unfortunate comrade, and there we stood until the following day until almost noon. We refused to go to work or do anything else until they came to remove the body. He, of course, knew nothing in death, but his memory deserved to be remembered, so we showed him the respect and dignity that had been stolen from him as we joined in this simple act of human and Christian solidarity.

The words of the reeducator, trying to justify what happened, were offensive and enraged even the most humble and quiet of prisoners. There were several very aggressive verbal exchanges, so to avoid greater evils and because there was nothing else we could do, a strike was declared against any talking for three days. No one would utter a phrase or answer questions any of the guards or officials might pose—not even a word or sound. Three companions went on hunger strike for a week. The prison authorities responded by suspending one of the three meager food rations per day for a full week.

The situation became very tense, and I was seriously concerned. But somehow God directed events so that there were no more personal misfortunes in this terrible crisis we had lived through. What happened showed us all once again the fragility of human existence and the manifest need we have as men and women to know God and have a personal relationship with Him.

This situation proved favorable to having more personal conversations with some of the prisoners with whom I had not been able to minister individually, and many approached me with questions about life, death, and the hope of resurrection. In this providential way, the Word of God continued finding its way into the hearts of those brave prisoners of conscience.

Chapter 17

Checkmate to the Pastor

*Then I returned and considered all the oppression that is done under the sun:
And look! The tears of the oppressed, but they have no comforter—on the side
of their oppressors there is power, but they have no comforter.*
—Ecclesiastes 4:1

*I said in my heart, "God shall judge the righteous and the wicked,
for there is a time there for every purpose and for every work."*
—Ecclesiastes 3:17

Several very tense weeks passed. We inmates barely communicated with those hostile guards, and the reeducator obviously felt insulted by his failure to command the attention he thought he deserved from the prisoners. After all, wasn't *he* the reeducator, for *he himself* had been educated in the infamous Schools of Revolutionary Instruction? Was *he* not a superior product of Marxism and Leninism, and had *he* not been commissioned to "enlighten or eliminate" those degenerates who in their "small-mindedness" only wanted to bring back the past? But the revolution, in its great benevolent wisdom, had commissioned *him*—the cream of the new society—to redeem us from our abysmal ignorance or make us disappear.

The challenge

Of those who remained in the farm group after the farce of a "graduation" for the undercover informers, not one of us had signed on to the infamous Rehabilitation Plan. The scheme to draw us in through the scientific game championship also seemed destined to fail. But that evening Ramon and Antonio threw the lieutenant an unexpected challenge: "If you're still interested in the chess tournament, we have a proposal. You decide who is going to represent your so-called new man, and we will choose one to fight for us," said Ramon. Antonio then explained the conditions, "The tournament will be held here in the mess hall. There will be as many games as necessary, but only one game per night. The champion will be the first to win three games, but those ending in a draw won't count. We insist on calling this the 'Chess Tournament in Memory of Andres Peralta.' That is our proposal, and if you disagree with these conditions, then that's that."

"Who will play for you?" asked the lieutenant.

"It will be the teacher," Antonio replied in a calm voice.

The proposal was bold; all of the logical reasoning one could rightfully expect from our political prisoners went into it. We didn't have many options to fight back, but here was a plan designed to vindicate our position and to honor the memory of one of our companions who had been taken out by the enemy force.

The lieutenant understood the significance of this challenge. The proposition wasn't exactly according to his original strategy, and it was likely his superiors would have considered it too politically risky, but he was so full of himself and convinced of his superiority that he did not hesitate to accept the challenge. "Well then, your teacher will have to face me!" he retorted. "Call the tournament whatever you want; it doesn't matter to me." Obviously, he figured that even this prisoner initiative would produce the results he was going for and would get his strategy back on track. In his mind, everything seemed optimal: *The end justifies the means once again. And no matter how pumped up these losers might feel, they don't stand a chance against someone like me. They're going to get so trounced that they won't forget this lesson for a very long time!* This is how he carried on in his hollow conversations leading up to the big game; clearly he was psyching himself up with the self-assurance that everything was going to turn out gloriously for him. For an added benefit, the arbiter for the match would be his colleague, the political commissar.

The scientific game

The day came, and everything was set for the battle that would take place on a board of sixty-four squares.

First, a little background explanation for those who are unfamiliar with this discipline: chess is a game for two players. You could say it's a game of war belonging to the same family as *xiangqi* (Chinese chess) and *shogi* (Japanese chess). It is believed that they both originated from *chaturanga,* which was practiced in India in the sixth century A.D.[1] It is considered not just a game but an art, a science, and a mental sport, not dependent on luck or on any mechanistic advantages to influence the outcome.

Although it is believed that learning to play chess can be useful as a way of developing the intellect, I am more in agreement with the old Latin adage "What nature does not give, Salamanca does not lend." (To put it in colloquial English: If you have no natural smarts, you're not going to pick up much in college.) And that first night the poor reeducator showed a terrible lack of common sense in his haste to put the pastor into check, with all the double symbolism that implied. He opened the battle by playing the white pieces, clearly intending to checkmate me speedily with a classical assault. In his vain mind, he thought everything was going to be easy; after all, he was facing a mere prisoner and even more to his opponent's disadvantage was his backward religious mind. On the other hand, he was a lieutenant, a reeducator, a splendid "new man" formed by the revolution to guide the nation into its glorious socialist future! So when he moved pawn 4 to open up for the king's bishop, I responded with the corresponding black pawn. When he continued to develop his strategy, I could clearly see how it would play out—it was elementary. What the reeducator had in mind was to align the queen and bishop in cooperation to attack the f7 square, which is the weakest point in proximity to the king, having no other defense. Wishing to show off, the lieutenant acted like a beginner and failed to note that I had positioned a black knight in the correct defensive position. He chortled delightedly and moved his queen to f7, so proud of himself and announced, "Checkmate, silly little pastor!" I jumped with my black knight and took out his queen to the utter dismay of the lieutenant, and the referee swore at him. I launched my offensive and, in less than twenty minutes, announced in a firm and solemn tone: "In memory of Andres Peralta, checkmate to the reeducator." It turned out that he wasn't as skilled as he boasted. Or maybe he was, and God wanted to place the man in my hand so that Heaven's plan could develop in my life of service to the other prisoners. I got up and left to avoid any possible conflict, because the man was furious and the prisoners jumped for joy, shouting and clapping like children.

Political failure

It goes without saying that the tournament ended right there, because the boastful man, his pride humiliated, ordered all the sets of the scientific game confiscated that very night. He never again showed his face at the penitentiary farm, but we learned that he had been punished for having committed what in those days in Cuba was called a "political failure." It's not hard to imagine what that failure was! Sergeant G. later let me know that differences arising between the reeducator and the political commissar led the higher prison administration to punish this loser.

That is how the Lord vindicated His humble, impugned children and rescued us from the dreaded reeducator. It was truly surprising, and it gave us some relief for a time.

---

1. See *Wikipedia*, s.v. "Chess," last modified September 11, 2016, https://en.wikipedia.org /wiki/Chess.

Chapter 18

The Arrival of My Firstborn

When you eat the labor of your hands, you shall be happy,
and it shall be well with you. Your wife shall be like a fruitful vine in the very
heart of your house, your children like olive plants all around your table.
Behold, thus shall the man be blessed who fears the LORD.

—Psalm 128:2–4

It was the fourth month of my imprisonment when Heaven sent the first of the two greatest gifts my wife and I have received in our lives—our first child! This experience was the upscale of joy and gratitude but also simultaneously the downscale of sadness and helplessness. Nevertheless, when all is said and done, the blessing far exceeded the hurt. Those were very intense, very happy moments but also very distressing; it was as if heaven and earth touched at that indefinite point of my existence.

He came into this world, albeit in an enslaved country, on August 28, which is the hottest month of the year in those latitudes. This little bundle would become one of the greatest lovers of freedom and justice I have known; my firstborn would one day become Pastor José H. Cortés Jr. He is not just a continuation of my given name and my family name or merely an extension of my ministry; he has become a young man beloved of God in his own right. He was, at the time of his birth, and will remain so, as long as I live, the great motive for my gratitude and healthy pride. He gave me an amazing boost to go on living and struggling through the hardships and sorrows of my situation.

I, of course, had not received any previous notice, and many hours had already gone by since the baby was born. Two prison guards, armed with AKM assault rifles, came to where I was at in the back of the barracks, and one of them announced, "We have orders to take you to the hospital. Your wife has had complications in childbirth, and at the request of your mother, the head official and Sergeant G. have authorized a pass."

"But how is she?" I asked.

"We know nothing; we only have orders to take you under guard. So hurry up; what are you waiting for? You have no hair to comb!"

As we went through all the annoying formalities to leave the penitentiary, it struck me as interesting that they were going to do the same thing in my case as they had done with my two friends a couple of years earlier: we would go by public transportation, with the two armed guards carrying assault rifles as if guarding a dangerous offender or as if escape was even a remote possibility. Sergeant G. was by the exit, and in a low, benevolent tone, he said to me, "I am sorry, my son. I could not do otherwise."

I responded, "Thank you, Sergeant. I will never forget your help!" And so it has been; I will always bless this good man.

"Real criminals are never transported on public buses," he explained later on my return, "this is only done with certain individuals, to make them feel publicly shamed." In my case, they used the opportunity to try to demoralize a pastor who had been preaching publicly in the city. It was part of their strategy to demonize those whom they considered enemies of the revolution.

But for me, none of that was of any importance. I was totally indifferent to their notions, and this public shaming did not disturb me in the slightest. No Communist government can demonize a servant of the Most High God.

In the maternity hospital

That day, which I remember well, was a Saturday, and at 1:00 P.M., when we entered the maternity hospital, I walked with my head held high and my guards behind. There were literally hundreds of friends and brothers, all the way from the hospital's entrance to the room where my wife was lying with our baby in her arms. Some folks hugged and kissed me; some laughed; and others wept with joy to see me again. Not one of them was ashamed of me! Everyone showered me with their love; for this reason, I love the brotherhood of the church. They stood with me and did not betray me during the entire ordeal and throughout all the years of my ministry and life. They have been family to me and my great blessing.

What a moment that was! The Good Lord showed me His mercy. That day I held my little son in my arms for the first time! That was all that mattered. The delivery had been difficult, but thank God my wife was out of danger! The excitement of seeing the two of them wiped away all my sorrows. The baby was strong, healthy, and beautiful. After all, he was my son, right? Celita, though very sore, was radiant in her motherhood, and my soul was comforted when I could kiss her forehead and stroke her hair. She could not yet get out of bed; but even so, those were moments of pain mingled with happiness, which we can never forget. Even now it brings tears of joy when we talk about that day.

My admiration for that sweet woman rises beyond the stars of heaven. With such patience and dignity she suffered through our time of separation, punishment, and undeserved abandonment. Celita, although she was always very tender, knew how to face the trial and resist this horrendous storm with great strength. Although our pastoral salary was suspended during that time when it was needed the most—honestly, I have never been able to find valid reasons for this miserable action—she never complained; instead, she stretched our humble savings to meet the needs that the arrival of a child represented. She knew how to take care of our infant son and protect our treasure in an economy as difficult as that.

Let me share with you an incident that took place about a month before the baby was born. There was a knock on the door by the chief of the Committee for the Defense of the Revolution (which is a group of busybodies who are responsible for monitoring everything that happens in their neighborhoods, in order to denounce anyone who violates the rules imposed by the government). This individual, who coincidentally was a lieutenant in the repressive forces of the government, came to the house where we lived and wanted to put up a sign saying, "My Happy Beautiful Home Joins in the Celebration of July 26th" (the date of the attack on the Moncada Barracks, taken as a symbol of the emergence of the revolution). When the visitor told my wife the reason for his call, she courageously confronted him in public view of numerous spectators and said, "How can you possibly think my house is happy and beautiful when your revolutionary government has imprisoned my husband unjustly? Forget it! You're not putting up any such poster here, and if you do, I'll rip it down!" The man left in an angry state. That's my wife, sweet and strong like sugar cane!

Back to the penitentiary

One of the guards said, "Your visiting time is up; we have to return to prison." What a difficult moment that was. It was like tasting honey and then having to eat bitter wormwood. They gave me only a few minutes, and then I had to say Goodbye and leave behind what I loved the most in life.

But those moments gave me the strength to keep fighting. The arrival of my little child, whom we dedicated to God even before he was born, confirmed the certainty and the hope that life would continue in God. My wife gave him my name, and I signed the birth certificate with two armed guards at my back as witnesses. I felt so very proud and blessed; the Lord Almighty was with me.

We returned to the penitentiary. When the prisoners began to hug and congratulate me, it felt like I was waking up from a wonderful dream, leaving me with the divine certainty that it was true and that it would be fulfilled to the letter. And so it was! Hope does not disappoint. It is a virtue of heavenly origin. Never lose it!

Chapter 19

A Sad Symbolism

"And you shall know the truth, and the truth shall make you free."
—John 8:32

To be set free from prison in Cuba is somewhat symbolic. Of course, it is amazing to feel the breeze and the sunshine once again on your face, and better yet, to behold the eyes of your wife, even if they are sad, and the smiles of your innocent children day by day. But the degree of pain and frustration experienced by those living under dictatorships—governed by individuals who believe they are (and so *they are*) the owners of lives, jobs, houses, and land; who perpetuate themselves in power indefinitely; and who destroy the dreams of generations of human beings—is beyond all limits. It is just too shameful. I would agree with the philosophy of many political prisoners, some of them locked away almost from the year of the triumph of the revolution: "What do you suppose you will find on the outside? *Set free?* That's a myth! You will only be moving from a locked fortress with bars, a small prison, out into the island of Cuba, a big prison, surrounded by shark-infested waters on all sides." The lack of freedom and self-determination is suffocating, and God does not want that. God wants all men and women to be free, respected by and respectful of their peers.

In the "big prison"
When I left prison, I went out profoundly transformed; something changed within me. I was sensitized more deeply to those who suffer, no matter what their political or religious affiliation. I could also see more clearly than ever the peculiar condition of human beings. I returned to my normal pastoral responsibilities in the church, but I was never the same. The school of suffering had taught me how to face difficulties with greater trust and assurance and how to draw closer to those going through pain. I felt a greater call to protect my "brothers." But at the same time, I also sensed the need to confront the furious wolves and unmask and confuse the agents of Satan. Since that experience, I think I've become better equipped as a pastor to fulfill my sacred ministry, and

this has been extremely valuable to me. I would not wish any human being to have to experience what I faced, but none of us can erase what life has dealt us.

Being discriminated against, or being called a "worm," a "scourge," and similar epithets, is part of the daily bread of those who do not subdue their faith or ideology to that of the governing system. Access to better-paying jobs and acceptance in recognized professions are options open only to the party faithful. Many of those considered as believers have compromised their faith; for the sake of the benefits of the revolution, they are willing to hide their religious affiliation. My wife, who had made her career in education and was an excellent teacher and school principal, was removed from her job based on the incomprehensible argument that a religious person was unfit to educate the new generations. But hers was not an isolated case, as in those days almost all educators who would not renounce their faith were purged from the education system to prevent them from corrupting the students. What a shameful absurdity! The influence of a Christian teacher can be great and a very worthy example for our children. In the words of the distinguished educator José de la Luz y Caballero: "Anyone can teach, but only those who live the gospel can educate."

During all these past years, we have sadly witnessed that forgetting those principles inevitably leads to backwardness, poverty, corruption, and ultimately the breakdown of society. Today we see the sad reality of a ruined country. Some have asked me, "Aren't things going right over there?" The answer is an emphatic No! "Isn't it true that they have granted concessions and liberties?" The answer is a categorical No—to be half free is not freedom!

Things will be fine over there, or anywhere in the world, when dictators are gone forever.

But enough philosophizing, since these reflections are open to debate. Let's return to the memories and facts of real life, elements that are indisputable and sometimes can teach us more than mere theoretical classroom lectures at any university. People can disagree with my way of thinking or my ideals; but in the face of what one has lived through, those who have no such experience do well to remain silent.

"You are going to Las Villas"

One morning, quite unexpectedly, Pastor Rafael Rodriguez, the president of the delegation (church association or conference) of Pinar del Río, called me into his office and informed me of important news. "José, we have been talking with Pastor Nicolas Bence and with the leaders of the national association [union conference], and we all believe a change will be very healthy for you and your family. Therefore, we are sending you to the association of Las Villas, and Pastor Ivan Diaz de Villegas will come take your place here in Pinar del Río." So it was that a few weeks later, we said Goodbye to our churches in the west of the island as well as to our parents and relatives, loaded our humble belongings aboard Brother Ramiro Cruz's old truck, and headed to our new destination of Las Villas, the central province of the island of Cuba.

Remembering the experiences lived together with our dear and unforgettable church members, whom we were leaving behind, and thinking of their afflictions still touches my heart. I also think of my friends and colleagues in the ministry from that time, back in the western part of the island, who each, to a greater or lesser degree, suffered persecution. Every one has a story to tell, and I hope one day those stories can all come to light. When thinking about all this, my heart is filled with feelings of gratitude. They were very good friends. We never met again as a pastoral team, and I doubt it will happen in this present world. But God has been and will continue to be with us all.

My prayer is that God blesses us all, wherever we are and whatever our situation!

Unforgettable experiences

Las Villas was not a strange, new place for me, as it was where I had gone for my college studies at the then-famous Colegio Adventista de las Antillas. It was the jewel of the church in that part of the world. This prestigious institution of higher education was where many young people came to learn—not only Cubans but people from all the Caribbean islands, Central and South America, as well as many other countries around the world. What a splendid college that was! It truly *educated the mind, the hand, and the heart*. It was my alma mater, a monument to education and faith. It was a beautiful home where everyone studied, worked, worshiped, and developed harmoniously. Even now, as I write these lines, many wonderful memories come rushing back into my mind very vividly, with all the colors and sounds. I can almost see before my eyes happy expressions on the faces of those pretty young women and young men. I hear their joyous laughter and chatter while they pass down the hallways on their way from one class to another. Echoing in my ears are strains of singing from those quartets that seemed to spring up as if by magic in every corner of the campus and in the dormitory. How can I forget waiting in line during the cheerful dining hours when we partook not only of food but also of Christian fellowship? I remember the smell of the freshly cut grass and the fragrance of the garden and the wild flowers on that beautified campus. I could never erase from my memory the ringing bell that called the faithful to vespers, the sound of our voices raised in great congregational music in the college chapel, or singing the magnificent "Hallelujah Chorus"—my tongue would cleave to my palate before I could forget that!

But the scene changes. Who among us there that day can forget when Hart Dávalos stormed in with his henchmen and their stench of tobacco? They desecrated our grounds, traipsed up onto the chapel platform at our college, and called an emergency meeting to tell us openly that we had to leave and abandon our school. We had to get out because now this institution, with all the buildings and all the farm implements, belonged "to the people" and not the church. As if we the students, teachers, and the church had not been part of "the people." Historically, this was a second intervention. Some years before there had been a more brutal and intimidating threat of closing the institution, but this second intervention was conclusive and irreversible. In the end, they did nothing with the property: the buildings were simply abandoned; the chapel left empty; the place became a haven for birds and bats. And there they are to this day, December 24, 2015. Those dear old buildings are now in ruins—just like the whole country—a wreck without a future, under the same system! If you want to verify this, visit Cuba, and go to kilometer 8 on the road to Camajuaní. There you will see what was once the famous Colegio Adventista de las Antillas; the ruins speak for themselves, and they will make you cry.

The power of Jesus

What a sweet experience it was to pastor the churches of Santo Domingo and Manacas; so many victories the Lord gave us in those parts. The first and most impacting triumph was the healing and deliverance of a beloved young man who suffered in the clutches of fallen angels. He had been taken to hospitals near and far, which treated him as if he were insane; but that was not his problem. When doctors and psychiatrists asked him, "What is your name?" He would answer, "Lucifer!"

"And where do you live?"

"Among the stones of fire." His voice was deep and resonated in an eerie way.

Warning! Many sincere believers, though lacking any knowledge of the subject—including some pastors, priests, and so-called exorcists—misdiagnose people suffering from mental illnesses, such as dissociative identity disorder (formerly known as multiple personality disorder) or schizophrenia, as being demon possessed. My humble advice: Do not play with these things if you are not trained to do so. It is necessary to refer such cases to the appropriate professionals; otherwise, you could inflict additional harm to a patient or confuse a believer who really does need professional help.

But in this case I that share with you, it was the reverse situation. The testimony of pastors and family members, which was given to the doctors and hospitals where he was taken for observation, was truly ghastly. Much time went by, and yet nothing could be done for him. But he was not crazy; he was tormented by demonic spirits that became very violent and terrifying. On one occasion, this young man violently shook Pastor Ara's Volkswagen minibus while being taken to the hospital; at other times, he tossed into the air the well-built men who tried to subdue him; and he broke down with his own hands the interior walls in his parents' house. There were times when our beloved and respected Pastor Cols traveled from another province to pray for him, and those were the only occasions when he would calm down. The demon in the house knew when the pastor was arriving at the bus station and would shout out: "Here comes this man of God to disturb me!" The devil would become dormant; but after the pastor left, it would return with a vengeance, shrieking, "I have dug myself in here!"

That was my welcome to the new district! One evening this young man's dear sisters sent me this message: "Pastor, please, do not come to visit us! Our brother is very violent. For two days, he has been waiting for you with a pitchfork in his hand. He does not sleep, will not eat, hasn't bathed, combed his matted hair, or shaved for many days, but he says he is waiting for you. When he lies down briefly, he keeps that pitchfork on his chest. The whole neighborhood is terrified. We are afraid that something terrible will happen!"

To be honest, I shuddered. I had on a couple of occasions dealt with cases of this nature, but nothing quite like this. I asked other pastors in the district who had dealt with the case what they recommended I should do, but they were not encouraging. They all advised me not to go anywhere near the house of this dear family, and no one offered to accompany me if I decided to do so. I thought of Pastor Cols, but he was conducting an evangelistic campaign in the eastern part of the country for the following six weeks. What to do? I went to my Bible and prayerfully began to review the cases that Jesus and His disciples faced that were similar to this one. I also reread the texts about the sons of Sceva and their ghastly failure. The evil spirit answered those seven men:

"Jesus I know, and Paul I know; but who are you?"
Then the man in whom the evil spirit was leaped on them, overpowered them, and prevailed against them, so that they fled out of that house naked and wounded (Acts 19:15, 16).

Two paths before me

I had only two paths before me: call the conference president and ask to be relieved of my duties or risk myself in the holy name of Jesus. During that night of study and prayer, two important truths were reaffirmed in my mind. First, that the power comes from Jesus, not from me! And second, "This kind does not go out except by prayer and fasting" (Matthew 17:21).

I decided to fast and pray through the night. When dawn came, I put my trembling hand in the Lord's hand and set out to fulfill my ministry. What an experience that was! When I was nearing the family's house, there came the three sisters and mother to meet me. "Please, don't go near the house!" they warned. "He knows you are coming and is very aggressive."

I replied, "Come, let's enter in the name of Jesus!" When I got closer, I saw a nightmarish scene: the dining and living room walls were destroyed as if by a hurricane! Above the wreckage, there was this very tall, strong young man, letting out the most horrifying shrieks, jumping high in the air, and brandishing a pitchfork like a warrior ready to attack his enemy. But something I noticed right away gave me a sensation of security; though he jumped and shouted ferociously, he didn't move in my direction as if to run me through. We advanced to the middle of the living space, and I said to the four women that we should kneel down. They were crying in fear, and I was tempted to get out of there but made myself stay. I don't know if you ever do this, but on that occasion I kept my eyes wide open as I prayed. My heart was even more widely open to God in total submission. Do you know what *total submission* means? It means that we are nothing but dust in the hands of God. Flashbacks from other times of danger came into my thoughts. I remembered past problems that were far bigger than me, and I recognized that I am nobody and deserve nothing. Then, surrounded by four desperately weeping women, I raised my voice and, inspired (at least I think so) by the Holy Spirit, cried out, "Dear God, I will not fight with the devil. I cannot. Who am I?"

At that moment, the wild young man stood tall and laughed with a horrible resonance. He held his pitchfork high and shrieked, "Look, companions, I have them cornered. The little pastor is kneeling down and won't come and face me!"

Then I cried out, from deep within myself, a simple and agonizing prayer: "Lord, today I just want to ask You one thing, that once and for all You heal him. I don't want to see this dear young man like this anymore, under Satan's control. I ask this not on my merits but by the powerful merits of Jesus, who died on the cross to give us freedom. Amen!"

Miracle of miracles! Before my astonished eyes, the young man fell to the ground as if struck by an invisible power; the pitchfork was flung from his hand; the raucous laughter and defying voices ceased. The Creator of the angels had subdued the devil once again, and the young man lying on the ground shuddered helplessly before the power of God. He was foaming at the mouth, but this gradually vanished and his faculties returned to normal.

For this dear family, those were indescribable moments. We gathered around his trembling body, cleaned his face, and that was when I dared to take him by the hand and say, "Come on, you can get up now. Jesus has freed you forever." We shared a big hug! We all cried with joy, for we had just witnessed the glory of God! Then I realized how much the young man needed to take a bath and tactfully suggested, "Go enjoy a nice warm bath, and put on some nice clothes because we have some things we need to do." What a testimony that was! We headed down the street like two friends normally would do, and the whole neighborhood watched us in disbelief. I took him to a barbershop to get his hair cut. To this day, I can't help but continue to thank God for that miracle of liberation. That young man became more than a friend; he is now like a son to me. During the following weeks, he rebuilt with his skilled hands everything he had destroyed in their home. All the love in his heart could now flow as from the fountain of living water, available to all who come to Christ and drink freely. Jesus freed him, and then all the beauty of a Christian character was manifested in him who had once been enslaved by the powers of darkness.

From that time on, he accompanied me as we did missionary work; we sang and played violin duets in church. He spent many hours working with me in rebuilding the church at Santo Domingo. I never had a more loyal and reliable disciple. Since then, he has been very close to my heart. What a joy to be able to talk with him two or three months ago when he came to visit Florida and called me. He is happy and has his own family now. God's work was complete in him; the enemy has never again been able to take control of him. God answered that simple prayer claiming the merits of the Savior Jesus. I have been careful not to mention his name in respect to his and the family's privacy; but when you read this book, dear family, know that I love you very much and that you are and always will be in my prayers. You are part of my spiritual family!

Chapter 20

The Largest Fine in the History of Cuba

Rejoicing in hope, patient in tribulation, continuing steadfastly in prayer;
distributing to the needs of the saints, given to hospitality.
Bless those who persecute you; bless and do not curse.

—Romans 12:12–14

It was in those days that the Communist Party decided to put an end to the church through financial stratagems, and a law was passed ordering the church to pay certain taxes, which had never existed before but were now to come into effect immediately. The money allegedly owed amounted to several hundred thousand pesos. The law was compulsory as well as retroactive. Our leaders had just thirty days in which to comply.

This was a low blow to be sure. The government knew how much money the church had in its bank accounts and the value of all its land and building assets, so they "very generously" suggested we make a down payment by turning over to them the property and buildings of the national association and all of the provincial offices (local conferences). For the balance yet owed, we could cover that cost by ceding to them ownership of all of our local church buildings. In other words, the church would become the property of the Communist government. It was almost a slam dunk for them!

God's people respond

What the government ignored was the fact that the church is God's—it is the apple of His eye—and God's people respond amazingly in times of crisis. We turned to God in prayer and fasting. At the national level, the denomination's administration sent a message to all churches in the country and set an appointed day for congregations to gather a sacrificial offering that, it was hoped, would help save at least the local church buildings if not, by sheer miracle, the headquarters properties. This brazen challenge by the government seemed too big for a people subjected to exploitation and poverty for decades. Among our people in Cuba, there were no millionaires we could turn to for help, not even well-off middle-class families. All the businesses, shops, factories, hospitals, and theaters with their artists—absolutely everything—were owned by the revolutionary government and the Communist Party. Their next goal was to dispossess the church. We were a people of workers and peasants; the only wealth that existed was held by the revolutionary government, which had become and still is the owner of lives and property. The only millionaire was the commander in chief, with his millions in foreign banks. Those conditions have not changed. Basically, what we have is an enslaved people who have to *fight and invent*, according to the popular Cuban saying, in order to lift another bite of food to their mouths at mealtimes. This may seem impossible or an exaggeration, but it is the honest truth.

All the pastors renounced their wages

Those were several tension-filled and unforgettable weeks. Despite the grave concern among the members, there were also moving testimonials. All of us pastors responded immediately, giving up our monthly salaries for as long as necessary. Without delay, the brothers and sisters, members of the church, did the same by donating their very livelihoods. I personally saw elderly retired folks bringing their meager pensions to the church treasury. It touches me still to remember the little children selling their few toys so that they could take some coins to give for this rescue.

And do you know what? That entire abusive fine was paid in full! All the church buildings and offices, national and provincial, were saved; and besides that, enough money came in to keep operating. The people of God saved their church from the clutches of the enemy! The church today exists and continues to grow in the midst of struggle and trials. The church marches on, stopping only long enough to preach and baptize.

Dear readers, a people like this deserves to be recognized by history! These people deserve to be mentioned! I don't know why we have lingered so many years to bring these testimonies to light. I recriminate myself for not having done so before this. But today I say to you, our church brothers and sisters, the Christians in Cuba, along with other people suffering similar circumstances: you are recognized by your spirit of love and sacrifice. I want the whole world to know. May God bless each and every one of you, who have given everything and more for the cause of the gospel of Jesus Christ.

Chapter 21

Times of Madness and Barbarism

Do not be overcome by evil, but overcome evil with good.
—Romans 12:21

To produce a complete compilation of all the twisted and ridiculous things that went on during this period in the history of Cuba would be a thankless and depressing task, and of course, to try to point the finger of blame at all those who share in the guilt would be senseless. Besides, that is not the purpose of this book, which only means to touch here and there on the island's political situation and its current masters as these enter into controversy with religious values—nothing more.

That being the case, why then do we get into the Mariel boatlift saga? Well, read on and you will discover the connection.

A grave error

One of the gravest errors of the Cuban dictatorship, right from the beginning, has been its insistence that the church and genuine Christianity are the enemies of social progress. This working of religion into the equation as a cause for social and economic failure has led the revolution to take unfortunate actions with dire consequences. Acting on that faulty premise, the government has tried unsuccessfully to reduce or eliminate the influence of the church at any cost. While devious and sometimes even hysterical, their strategies are ultimately going to fail because they have foolishly undertaken to do battle with a powerful force already shown to be far more than a match for them. The church, though made up of human beings, is linked to a heavenly government that will ultimately prevail. Some may not believe this, but history reveals the folly of rulers who thought they could win in such an unequal contest. In Cuba, just as in China and in the defunct Soviet bloc of socialist countries, it has been demonstrated that Christianity not only weathers the storms of oppression but grows stronger than ever before.

Learn this all you megalomaniacs of any tendency, when the last of this world's dictators have passed from the scene and vanished into nothingness, Jesus Christ will still reign on the eternal throne of heaven and in the hearts of His faithful, because He is our God and the Creator of the universe.

The pressure-cooker syndrome

It has been the Cuban Revolution's mode of operation, as in other countries with similar systems, to reduce internal pressures and political tensions by eliminating opponents instead of listening to their reasoning. Cuban leaders have not been able to listen to reason. They have acted as if they were the exclusive owners of the island, and all those who do not think as they do have basically three choices before them: they can die; they can live as prisoners; or finally, the best plan, they can leave the country. With this stark set of options before the people, the masters of the island remain in power unopposed.

To the leaders' benefit, they have very close by a great and powerful nation that they never cease to blame for all of their internal woes and fiascos. Everything bad that happens is "the fault of imperialism" and not their own mismanagement.

This other country has been a blessed haven for harassed Cubans while at the same time a tremendous financial boon for the dictatorship because every refugee fleeing north has dear family left behind who need financial assistance. This faithful, generous flow of funds to the island has been constant. By means of government manipulation of the dollar–peso rate of exchange, the Castro government has been able to swell its coffers, giving the Cuban people soft pesos for hard dollars. In this way, both the hardworking refugees and the needy families back home on the island continue to be abused. Additional abuse by the authorities in Cuba stems from restrictions imposed on what is allowed into the country from Cubans abroad; this affects foodstuffs, medicines, clothing, and so on. The Castro government is always looking for ways to squeeze more from the Cuban community in the United States. But enough said about this matter; it is too ignoble what the exiles have to put up with when all they are trying to do is help their families back on the island.

Times of madness

The Mariel boatlift, or Mariel Exodus, was an open escape valve to relieve the supertense situation that existed in Cuba at the time.

Just in case you do not know what the Mariel boatlift was all about, let me review the story for you in a nutshell: the Mariel boatlift was a mass movement of Cubans who left the port of Mariel in Cuba and came to the United States between April 15 and October 31, 1980. The origin of this exodus has to do with an assault made on the Peruvian embassy in Havana by a group of

Cuban civilians who commandeered a public bus to crash their way through the gates. Their goal was to enter the premises and seek political asylum. During the assault, a security guard, Pedro Ortiz Cabrera, was shot while protecting the embassy. Ortiz died on the way to a hospital. In response to that, Cuban president Fidel Castro threatened the Peruvian embassy (a country with which relations were already quite tense) if they refused to hand over the Cuban men. The embassy refused Castro and gave the gate-crashers diplomatic protection. Fidel then made good on his threat and announced on public media that anyone who wanted to seek asylum in the embassy could do so without reprisal. The response of the population exceeded by far what the Cuban government anticipated, and within days, more than ten thousand Cubans took refuge in the embassy gardens. Given this situation, and needing to find a way out of this dilemma, Fidel Castro authorized Cuban exiles in Miami who wanted to collect their relatives to sail down to Cuba, dock their boats at the port of Mariel, which is west of Havana, and carry away all those they wanted, unimpeded by his military. According to the data, more than 125,000 Cubans left the port of Mariel.[1]

In response to this wave of migration, the Cuban government announced in the media that most of the dissidents were "undesirables" and were regarded as a "danger to society." While it is true that numerous common criminals were put on the departing boats, most of these so-called undesirables were very decent and honorable people. Also among those branded as undesirable and insulted as garbage and scum by the Cuban authorities were hundreds of thousands of religious folks who were harassed to leave the country. From my church in Santa Clara alone, they collected on that memorable Friday, and I remember very well, two buses, packed with my brothers and sisters—very worthy Christians, indeed, and good workers.

War of nerves

But the matter does not end there. A week later, on the following Sunday, the infamous Captain Bruno sent two soldiers in a military vehicle to inform me that my family and I were also selected to leave the country. My answer was blunt: "I will not leave this country until the last of the members of my church has gone!" They left me alone for the time being, but the next week a police car with flashing red-and-blue lights would park every night as near as it could on the street by the window where my wife and I slept. Obviously, it was to intimidate me with a war of nerves! I went out and berated the officers for this ridiculous tactic, but they were back again the following night. When I protested, they simply answered, "We're only following orders."

The terror of the proletariat

The cities convulsed day after day, and weeks of indescribable disorder befell Cuba; it was a "Reign of Terror of the proletariat."[2] Traffic on the streets was blocked by organized crowds; workers and employees had to go out and join the march, even during paid working hours, because they were under orders from their superiors to hit the street in support of the revolutionary government in its actions to hound all who were accused of being disloyal. But even amid so much disgrace, our Cuban sense of humor would slip out: "Good morning, Garbage! Leaving soon?" "I'm just fine, Piece of Scum! Wait and see!" We would laugh but really felt more like crying over all the mindless barbarism.

Can you imagine a government that is supposed to keep order and safeguard the integrity of its citizens allowing, encouraging, organizing, and inciting mobs to tear around peaceful neighborhoods, dragging people out of their homes violently? These victims were the very people the government wanted to deport because it considered them dangerous and antisocial. Then the mob would corral the despised "traitors" into a park or plaza where they could be fired upon with eggs from all sides. I sincerely believe that the enemies are not these so-called traitors but those who promote such disgrace.

As the pastor of the church at Santa Clara, I was an eyewitness in my own community to truly shameful scenes. But I must say that Santa Clara was not unique in this regard; the same crazy, abominable abuses were taking place all around the country.

By the central park, near the church, I saw many of those hoodlums shoving and dragging along with them people who had placards hung from their necks with derogatory slogans and profanity. It was painful to see those excesses, and the civil authorities and the police not doing anything to contain or mitigate the violence. They just shrugged their shoulders and said, smiling, "It's the violence of the revolutionary people."

The most sadistic people brought hard-boiled eggs to cause more pain to their victims. Chicken eggs break open and stain, but they also can bruise and cut the skin and hurt the eyes. Some of the people dared to ask with a touch of sarcasm where they got so many eggs to throw when it was practically impossible to buy them for food!

Acts of repudiation

"Acts of repudiation" became fashionable around the country. What were these acts all about? It was intimidation by organized rabble. These repressive groups came together, rioted, shouted horrible insults, and threw eggs and stones at the houses of those families disaffected by the regime. Children and women hid in fear; terrified older folks trembled. It seemed like a time of barbarism, and so it was. It was like a horror movie, full of rage and hate.

I remember one evening when the rabble came for my friend Tomás. They began to shout: "Worm! Garbage! Traitor!" Everyone in the house was very tense. What would happen? The people started throwing eggs and stones. But Tomás was and is a very courageous man and pastor. He opened the door, walked out, and, with his big preacher voice, bellowed, "I am not a traitor!" All were dumbfounded. "I have never been a Communist or had anything to do with you. Therefore, I have not betrayed you or anyone else! Please, enough! Go on home, calm down, and stop bothering others!"

Much to the surprise of Migdalia, Tomás's wife, and to the surprise of those of us who were there, the crowd dispersed but not before launching their last remaining eggs.

A clearer picture of this time takes shape for those who have never experienced anything like this, and the memories are refreshed for those who lived through these incredible events. It was the same in every part of the island of Cuba; truly despicable moments in the history of a nation, but at the same time, full of intense emotions for the players. Those were times of madness and passion, but God took care of us and gave us many victories; some of them were very significant in those difficult times.

---

1. See *Wikipedia*, s.v. "Mariel Boatlift," last modified August 18, 2016, https://en.wikipedia.org/wiki/Mariel_boatlift.

2. Karl Kautsky, *Karl Kautsky: Selected Political Writings*, ed. and trans. Patrick Goode (London: Macmillan Press, 1983), 122.

Chapter 22

Carrying Out a Great Work

Then I sent to him, saying, "No such things as you say are being done,
but you invent them in your own heart." For they all were trying
to make us afraid, saying, "Their hands will be weakened in the work,
and it will not be done." Now therefore, O God, strengthen my hands.
—Nehemiah 6:8, 9

These events passed, along with all the excitement of the days of Mariel and *El Mosquito* ("Cubans waiting to leave were jammed into a filth-strewn tent camp appropriately named *El Mosquito*"),[1] and the revolution's famous "prophets" announced the disappearance of the church in Cuba.

We now faced a different animal: individuals posing as new converts. But in reality, these were spies sent to report on our actions and see if there were any of a suspicious nature. This was nothing new, but at that time their numbers increased considerably. Because of their insecurity, dictators are always seeing phantoms where none exist. We went to church to worship God, not to stir up a counterrevolution or engage in politics. Again I say, the church is the house of God, but the government's leaders decided that we were enemies, and they chose to hold us in enmity. For years, they have treated and persecuted us as such. They have continually sent their paid or voluntary agents to mingle with us and keep the government informed of everything that goes on in the church. How bothersome these people can be! Several were infiltrators sent to report on every step I took, if I bought a brick or a bag of cement. Some were false brothers who did everything possible to try to neutralize our missionary work. They used various tactics and strategies, such as making heartless accusations against faithful members or initiating slanderous rumors in order to cause divisions in the congregation. Others came to draw away or demoralize new converts. They were like ravenous wolves in sheep's clothing; at other times, throwing off the sheepskin, they acted like the whores of Moab. The elders and I had to fight hard battles, but the devil did not prevail. The eyes of the Lord were upon His beloved church and upon me as pastor. We reorganized and got down to the work that was entrusted to us; God blessed us greatly and confused our enemies. What most irritated them was when one or another of their agents was touched by the power of the Holy Spirit and became genuinely converted, accepted Jesus Christ, confessed their sins, and repented. I particularly enjoyed those victories!

The church was in need of repairs and renovations. So a race against the clock began. We had to stack up the benches in a big pile to make room for some materials that couldn't be left outside. We wheeled in huge piles of sand and stone for work inside the sanctuary following the prayer service. I often had to preach my sermon in overalls, with my Bible in hand while standing on top of a pile of material. But we were very excited and grateful. The women got busy and took turns bringing in food for the workers, and in every way, God provided. We worked three shifts of eight hours each; it was an epic marathon of an experience. The government sold us some of the materials, but most of it God provided, just don't ask me how. Faith also moves mountains of concrete!

The heroes of the hour were once again our church members. We united as one to work each and every spare hour possible; the cooperation was tremendous. I can still see the sweaty but beaming faces of my fellow workmen: Brother Andres Mesa, a true titan; Jorge Diaz, a pastor today, but back then he was our first elder; Críspulo Pérez, a tireless deacon; the architect Juan Rodriguez, nicknamed the Rapid One; and, of course, our church youth who spiced up the long work hours with their songs and sometimes corny jokes: Daniel Vilas, Tony, Benjamin, and all the other anonymous heroes who for reasons of space aren't named.

Because we had no more land on the sides or the back of the church, we had to expand upwards, so we added a balcony, which expanded the capacity of the sanctuary. Two side balconies, an outdoor hallway, and a beautiful baptistry were also built. On the basement level, a hallway connected the pastor's office and the bathrooms. We redid the classrooms for the children and decorated them with beautiful fish tanks. Because our old pews were in bad shape, we replaced them with beautiful padded, theaterlike seating, which was upholstered in a red-wine color. These seats we acquired from our friends at the Jewish synagogue on Linea Street in Havana. We did everything we possibly could. Under those circumstances, it was something wonderful and extraordinary to behold. When we rededicated our remodeled church, we were all very tired but very happy. It was a great victory!

Unfortunately, someone paid for his magnanimity toward the church. One day I came upon the registrar of Associations in the central park of Santa Clara, and naturally I wanted to greet him with an expressions of thanks. With a nervous look on his face, he said, "Pastor, I cannot even stop to say hello. Please go your way. They are watching me closely; I'm sorry!" And he disappeared into the crowd. Later we learned that he had been dismissed from his post and sent on a mission as punishment. That's the way things are in that country. My insides still suffer when I think about those people and remember all that we lived through together and what they continue to have to put up with!

My dear and unforgettable church of Santa Clara! During and after that crisis, the church recovered; many new people were coming to our evangelistic campaigns; and we had good leaders in the congregation, a large group of wonderful youth, and very good music.

The love and contagious joy of that beautiful church family attracted people from the community in a special way; our membership doubled and continued to grow. One day I received the highest praise ever of my ministerial life when the first elder, a very spiritual and experienced man, came over to me after one of those grueling work days and said confidentially, "Pastor Cortés, I just want to say something: you were born to be a pastor!" Thank you for those touching words, Manolo, my dear brother, wherever you might be reading these words of gratitude. I believed what you said because it came from you, and I want you to know that beautiful expression has inspired me in good times and bad. I will never forget you; your dear Nonina, now resting in the Lord; nor the boys. And I will continue on with the help of God until the day of the Second Coming or until my last breath. I will remain a pastor, because as you said, I was born for that!

---

1. Juan O. Tamayo, "The Mariel Exodus: From Trickle to Tsunami," *Miami Herald*, April 17, 2010.

Chapter 23

The Doctor and the Street Sweeper

*He who dwells in the secret place of the Most High shall abide
under the shadow of the Almighty. I will say of the LORD,
"He is my refuge and my fortress; my God, in Him I will trust."*
—Psalm 91:1, 2

Sometime later I was called to pastor the great church of La Vibora (the Viper) in Havana. It was an exciting and interesting time. In the first evangelistic campaign we conducted in the spring, so many people came that the huge church was filled to capacity, and the crowd clustered at the front doors and side windows and even out on the sidewalks, which were very wide. This bothered the authorities, and they sent paramilitary cadres (mockingly called "little toads" behind their backs because of their faded green uniforms). These rude youth shoved and dispersed the outside crowds, who had come only because they wanted to hear the Word of God. These young people obeyed the powers of darkness, who were undoubtedly angry about the wonders that the Lord was working in the midst of the people.

The whole church was involved in small-group ministries; numerous households in the community discreetly opened to give Bible studies. The revolutionary government's law regarding "cults" prohibited Bible study outside the walls of a church, but we decided to "obey God rather than men" (Acts 5:29), and the church grew with dozens of new believers added to the church body. In my baptismal class, I always had more than 170 people in preparation for baptism; the class operated on a relay plan: as soon as a participant was baptized, a friend was brought in to fill that chair in the study group. These were very beautiful times, accompanied by great victories of faith and hope; but under the very repressive and intransigent government that did all it could to make the work of the church difficult, these were especially trying times for our new converts.

The experience of a medical doctor and street sweeper

During this time of deep spiritual emphasis, a young doctor began to attend our meetings. I was giving a series of talks on Bible prophecies at the time. This interested guest, whom we shall call Isaac Suarez to protect his identity, practiced in the National Hospital in Havana. He was an excellent physician, an extremely competent person, loved by his patients and coworkers. Isaac, moved by the love of God and the teachings of the gospel of Jesus Christ, opened his heart and became a happy Christian. I had the joy of baptizing him along with forty-three other believers one evening during Easter week. His testimony became known throughout the community as his joy and desire to share the truth were impossible for him to hide. Then something very wrong happened that never should have. The political leaders of the hospital retaliated against him. Let me remind you that all the hospitals, clinics, nursing homes, and other medical-related work in Cuba were owned and operated by the government, just like almost everything else. Their guidelines are dictated by the Communist Party, the only political party permitted in the nation. When they heard about Isaac's conversion, they immediately decided this was unacceptable; they would not tolerate a Sabbath-keeping Adventist forming part of their medical staff. This was a serious problem for the doctor because it was impossible for him to find employment in any other hospital in the country because they all operated under the same government criteria.

Dr. Suarez was very courageous, and he remains so, but he suffered considerably. It's not easy for a person, after making every effort required for a medical career—someone who studied for years in that demanding discipline and who loves this career—to end up losing everything just because of some arbitrary decision. Cases like this, which for some might seem remote and incomprehensible, demonstrate a lack of sensitivity and respect for the rights of others in systems such as this.

I decided to join forces with Dr. Suarez and naturally began praying and sending letters to the hospital administration, asking them to reconsider the case, but the answer was negative. We tried to contact the local authorities and that proved impossible. I asked for an interview with the directors of the regional medical administration, because it was the superior body. We presented a well-developed review of the case at that level, and the various individuals there seemed to understand and accept the validity of my arguments on a personal level, but the answer was always the same: "It is not in our hands." After numerous rejections and interviews with various individuals at different levels, we concluded from their recommendations that the only one who could authorize what we were seeking was the secretary general of the Communist Party in Havana Province. But getting an interview with this official was extremely difficult. Things were becoming even more difficult for Isaac and for me, but one of the things I've learned in this life is not to give up when I'm fighting for a just cause and not to be afraid of enemies, no matter how fearsome they might be. God is greater than all our problems, and He is more powerful than earth's most powerful leaders.

At that point, something unexpected happened that made me exclaim, "God save me from my enemies as well as from my friends!" The president of the national association of the church, a very dear and respected friend, called me to his office and began urging me to abandon the doctor's problem. The authorities had called his attention to this case with a warning that the pastor of the church of La Vibora could find himself in serious trouble if he kept on insisting about this "discrimination against Dr. Suarez." My response was, I confess, a bit disrespectful; but I don't think he held it against me. I said to him, "I am going to continue fighting for this young Christian doctor. I don't fear these abusive officials; if you fear them, buy yourself a dog!"

"I cannot back you in this," he replied. "If you want to cause trouble, don't count on me. Do you understand? You're alone in this." Leaving his office in the national association, I said sadly, "I already know that! But do not worry, I learned to be alone, very alone—but alone with God while I was in prison."

Interview with the secretary general

I finally got an interview with the most senior functionary in Havana, and the day arrived. It was a pity that the authorities did not allow me to bring Dr. Suarez, but I carried in my briefcase all the young doctor's credentials and copies of every letter we had sent during the process and all the negative responses we received from the different levels of the Ministry of Public Health. I also carried with me a second folder, just in case there was an opportunity to present it. (Oh my, but did that chance present itself!) This folder was well loaded with all the documentation of another unfortunate and shameful case, involving an old street sweeper—a faithful worker who had also been fired from his job because of his religion. This happened when he was just seven months away from qualifying for retirement benefits.

The secretary general received me in his austere but elegant office. To the right of his huge mahogany desk, the lovely flag of Cuba and a red flag with a hammer and a sickle were displayed, draped from two crossed staffs. Behind him on a high wall, hung three huge portraits: one of Vladimir Ilyich Ulyanov, a.k.a. Lenin, to one side, and to the other side, one of Karl Marx. Placed respectfully between them was the commander in chief. On the desk, between his telephone and his agenda book, there was a stone with an ubiquitous phrase engraved on it: Workers of the World, Unite.

The man opened with a certain degree of feigned cordiality, which seemed to me something like a cat playing with a mouse just before it delivers the fatal bite. He was quite aware of his authority, and he seemed sure of his philosophical superiority. It seemed that this interview was nothing more to him than one of those little acts of condescension that a great political personage occasionally granted to someone like me, an inconsequential clergyman who obviously needed to understand the revolutionary process better. His words, after a brief greeting, went immediately in that direction. He gave me a chance to briefly amplify the reason for my visit, which I had been required to write out when I requested the interview. He had already analyzed the matter, and I was merely there to receive the definitive answer: "Doctor Suarez should forget about those religious concepts that could interfere with his medical services to the population and simply fulfill his commitments to the revolution. It is as simple as that. No half measures!" He began to close the agenda book where he had his notes, as if to say, this is over.

At that precise moment, I fired back, "You know what? Here is something that is inconsistent with the principles of the revolution!"

"What are you saying to me?"

"That you do not respect the basic guidelines of the revolution!"

"Be very careful with what you are saying!" he warned defensively.

Then I returned to my attack, "We have studied in school that this revolution was carried out by the people and for the good of the people, to end discrimination against blacks, to end discrimination that oppresses the poor and women; but here we are now, establishing a new kind of discrimination—discrimination against religious folks!

"What you just said demonstrates that you support the outrage that the National Hospital and the Ministry of Public Health are committing against this young doctor, who was an excellent student and is now a very promising professional. You have expressed with full authority that Dr. Isaac Suarez cannot exercise his profession as a doctor, simply because he believes in God and practices his faith. It is abundantly clear that this is a case of religious discrimination."

"Look, Pastor; listen to me!" For the first time, he addressed me as a pastor, and I realized that I had hit him in a soft spot. Then he began to scratch his head and tried to justify what he had just said: "We are talking about a doctor! If this was about some other kind of worker, I could help you solve the problem; but with a doctor it is different."

"Why is it different?" I demanded. "Doesn't it seem to you that we've entered an era of witch hunts in which all who practice a religion or hold a different ideology are to be treated in this fashion? Is that social justice? For this, the blood of the martyrs was spilled? What can my children and all the youth of my church expect from this revolution if they decide to study medicine or some other university program?"

"Don't get upset!"

"Of course, I'm very angry with what you're saying. You people are mistreating and discriminating against religious folks in every situation where an opportunity presents itself for getting ahead, and it's just not right. It hurts."

The secretary general of the party did not expect quite so much forcefulness or my use of the revolution's own dialectic reasoning. With God's help, he was thrown off balance, and I didn't give him time to recover. Reaching into my briefcase, I pulled out the other folder and said, "Look at this other case! Brother Pineda is a humble man, a working man, who like many other believers has been mistreated. For years, the only job that he could get was street sweeping and collecting rubbish. No problem with that—it's an honest job like any other—but he has now been fired from his job for the same reason as the doctor! For religious reasons. And the most shameful thing about this is that you're doing him this wrong when he lacks only seven months to qualify for retirement. This is abuse heaped upon abuse!

"I have repeatedly called the regional office of community services, and the administrator will not receive me to have a conversation about this case. I have written three letters to this man who thinks he is—and, in fact, is—the 'king of garbage collectors,' and he simply denies me an interview. And there sits Brother Pineda at his age, no job, no money to support his family, and without his right to a retirement pension. Shall he go out and steal? Of course not! And he wouldn't because he's an honest, Christian man.

"Do you realize the levels to which we have fallen in this country? Please tell me! Where are we going to end up? What's next?"

The political leader fell silent; his face was as red as a tomato, and I thought I had probably gone too far. I hoped he didn't send me back to jail! But as my grandfather used to say, "What's done is done!" I prayed, "Lord, we're in Your hands!"

Finally, he decided to speak and said, "Pastor Cortés, you may leave now; I will contact you about the resolution of these issues."

I did not know whether to thank him or send him to hell, but I chose the former. I grabbed my briefcase and left.

Nearly a week went by. Meanwhile, the doctor, the street sweeper, the pastor, and the whole church of La Vibora were in intercessory prayer. I know the angels of heaven were working on the hearts of the adversaries because Alina Salgueiro, the secretary to the president of the delegation, called me urgently one day at midmorning. "Pastor Cortés, you have a phone call from the secretary general of the Communist Party in Havana!" I quickly grabbed the phone and immediately recognized the voice of the man speaking to me. God was at work and a modern miracle was occurring! With a cheerful voice, he said, "Pastor, everything has been resolved. Dr. Suarez can return to his regular work tomorrow at the National Hospital. And Mr. Pineda should also present himself on

Monday for his regular duties at the Department of Street Cleaning. He will be paid back pay for the weeks of lost work, and his position will be respected until the day of his retirement. Oh, and for what it's worth, for this and other situations, 'the king of garbage collectors' has been removed from office, and another person is taking over that responsibility."

I thanked him, warmly this time, for he seemed sincere. But I gave the glory to God who has never forsaken me, even when I had to face the very devil, who sometimes manifests himself in human form, while at other times humans manifest themselves as demons.

That was the last time I got to talk to the secretary general of the Communist Party of Havana. Afterward everyone was surprised by the news that this gentleman no longer continued in that high position as a political leader; he returned to managing a company in which he had previously worked. We never discovered the reason behind this move; it was not made public, but I seem to have an idea. There are still honest people who cannot put up with crass injustice! Just in case the much-appreciated former secretary general of the party gets to read this book, I'm praying for you—and I'd like to see you in the kingdom!

Chapter 24

There Is Hope for All

For the needy shall not always be forgotten;
the expectation of the poor shall not perish forever.
—Psalm 9:18

T here is hope for all. "God is no respecter of persons" (Acts 10:34, KJV); to Him all are equal; and He gives us the opportunity to be redeemed by grace, not by our merits. Learn this helpful equation:

$$S = GG + N.$$

Salvation is equal to the Grace of God plus Nothing more, period.

You may be guilty or innocent; you may have been in a prison or a high government seat. Nevertheless, every one of us, at some point in our lives, has been guilty to a greater or lesser extent, but that makes no difference to the love of God. You continue to be a human being, and that is what is most valuable to Him in this world. Your intrinsic value does not depend on where you are; it does not depend on the circumstances surrounding you; and it certainly does not depend on the people in power who may have control over certain aspects of your life. They might govern temporarily, but they do not have the power to define you. Above every other consideration, you are a son or daughter of God. Your Creator has assigned you a value that corresponds only to the work of His hands, as the prophet Isaiah rightly said:

But now, O Lord,
You are our Father;
We are the clay, and You our potter;
And all we are the work of Your hand (Isaiah 64:8).

The human being is the greatest wonder of creation, even though made of clay, because man and woman were made by God's hand, and God dearly loves

His handiwork. He is for us! He is our Creator and Redeemer! Our Refuge is the God of Israel!

If you feel diminished by the weight of your mistakes, if a sense of guilt drags you into the abyss, please understand that there is an outside force ready to come to your rescue, a heavenly power waiting for you to stretch out your hand to His already reaching hand so that He can lift you out of the hole and make you great.

God loves people who are honest and good, but He also loves very much those who have done wrong. He does not forget the convicts; please do not turn your back on those who have committed crimes. God loves many who should be in jail but still are out there doing harm, with impunity. Be wary and exercise caution, but do not curse them. It is true that crimes and human errors generally have human consequences that have to be admitted and repaid, often with punitive damages added, but above and beyond all that, is the love of God, which passes all understanding. I cannot understand how God can love people like us, like you and me, but—I have no doubt about it—He truly loves us! He gave the world the greatest proof of His love that ever could have been given when He sent "His only begotten Son, that whoever believes in Him should not perish but have everlasting life" (John 3:16). Let's brand these words with fire in our minds: "For God did not send His Son into the world to condemn the world, but that the world through Him might be saved" (verse 17).

The devil's job is to destroy the image of God in His creatures, but Jesus' work is to restore the lost image of God in every human being willing to accept Him. He will do for you what you cannot do for yourself and what no one else has the ability to do.

Today, His arms are open to you. Come! Never lose hope!

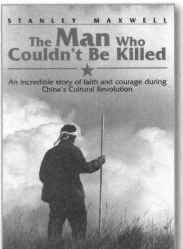
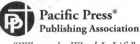